SO-BZE-660

Rd
2 –

BEHOLD, I STAND AT THE DOOR AND KNOCK

S. C. Biela

COMMUNION OF LIFE WITH CHRIST THROUGH MARY

Denver, CO

Nihil Obstat: Timothy J. McCarthy, J.C.L.
                   Vice Chancellor, Archdiocese of Denver
                   Censor Librorum

Imprimatur: +Most Reverend Charles J. Chaput, O.F.M. Cap.
                   Archbishop of Denver
                   August 23, 2004

Excerpts from the *New American Bible with Revised New Testament and Psalms* Copyright © 1991, 1986, 1970 Confraternity of Christian Doctrine, Inc., Washington, DC. Used with permission. All rights reserved. No portion of the *New American Bible* may be reprinted without permission in writing from the copyright holder.

Copyright © 2005 by S. C. Biela

Published by
In the Arms of Mary Foundation
P.O. Box 271987
Fort Collins, CO 80527-1987
E-mail address: inquiry@IntheArmsofMary.org
Website: www.IntheArmsofMary.org

For more information about the Foundation "In the Arms of Mary" or to obtain additional copies of this book, please visit us at our website (see back pages of this book for more details).

Translated by
Very Rev. Jaroslaw Zaniewski, Rector SS. Cyril and Methodius Seminary, MI

Edited by
Annette J. Higle   Michelle L. Curtis   Erin C. Rice
Anne Mary Hines   Joyce E. Pfaffinger

Cover and text design by
Ewa Krepsztul

Cover photo by
Réunion des Musées Nationaux / Art Resource, NY

This printing was made possible thanks to the generous financial support of Mr. & Mrs. Ludvik F. Koci in memory of Chuck and Connie. All they ask for in return are our prayers.

ISBN 0-9721432-3-8 (Softback)
ISBN 0-9721432-8-9 (Hardback)

First edition printed in the United States of America 2005

*I dedicate this book to our
Holy Father John Paul II, who so
urgently desires each heart to
open its door to Jesus Christ.*

CONTENTS

Theodore Cardinal McCarrick
Archbishop of Washington

I n his newest book, Slawomir Biela, one of the most prolific spiritual authors of our times, shared with us more of his deep insights. Once again, he returns to a reflection on the profound truths that are contained in the well known yet often overlooked passage from the Book of Revelation: "Behold, I stand at the door and knock. If anyone hears my voice and opens the door, [then] I will enter his house and dine with him, and he with me" (3:20). Throughout his work, which bears the title *Behold, I Stand at the Door and Knock*, Biela makes these words come to life, inspiring in the reader a deeper hunger to probe the truth about who God is and who we are, especially in our childlike relationship to Him. Once again, the author strongly emphasizes on each page of his work that the means to savoring this truth is humility. According to Biela, it is in and through our humility that we more clearly perceive the truth that we receive everything from God.

At the same time, the author also reminds the reader that the second part of this text from Revelation reminds us that God waits for us to assume the posture of the child in the Gospel (see Matthew 18:24). Meditating on this evangelical text, we humbly realize that Jesus is like a beggar who stands and knocks on the door of our hearts, waiting for us to respond so that He may give us love upon love, "grace upon grace" (John 1:16) – His Divine Everything. This reality challenges the reader's undivided attention and continually reminds us that humility does not focus on itself; rather, humility presents itself in a disposition oriented toward the reception of God's gifts.

Biela's words reflect those of His Holiness Pope John Paul II, who declares in his Apostolic Letter *Novo Millenio Ineunte*, that "it is fatal to forget that 'without Christ we can do nothing' (cf. John 15:5)." By considering and responding to Biela's reflections and insights into the nature and the consequences of a life of humility, we also respond to our Holy Father's urgent call to base our pastoral outreach and indeed our entire lives "on the primacy of Christ and union with him, the primacy of interior life and holiness." In both Part A: **Light of the Truth**, and Part B: **Childlike Humility**, the author of *Behold, I Stand at the Door and Knock* points out that the degree to which we will achieve the freedom to participate in God's life and thus make it possible for the supernatural life to unfold in our souls (see James 4:6), is determined by the degree to which we are humble.

Biela tells us that pride, the enemy of humility, is the chief terrorist of human freedom, peace, and happiness. He asserts that when we give in to pride, when we believe in our own self-sufficiency and self-importance, we choose to live the terror of darkness. Because pride is so filled with itself, it presumes that it does not need God. Biela reminds us that Christ most strongly denounces pride. He does not stop at stating, along the same lines of Dietrich von Hildebrand, that every virtue and every good deed become worthless if pride creeps into them.

Biela develops the teaching more fully in Part A: **Light of the Truth**. Here Biela presents and reflects on the scriptural image of the whitewashed tomb and suggests how we can allow God's healing light to show us different aspects of the interior state of our own souls. He assures his readers that by following the stages of spiritual life we are all led along the path to true freedom. We are led gradually to reject our illusory images of our own egotistical "I" so that we may be open to the only truth that is worthy of our fascination: The Divine *You.*

In Part B: **Childlike Humility**, the author develops the notion of spiritual childlikeness. He presents it as the most effective medicine for curing the darkness of prolonged discouragement or even despair that might be provoked by the hopeless and faith-deprived state of our whitewashed tombs. He teaches that this childlike posture allows us to be embraced more tightly in the arms of our Heavenly Mother, Mary, after each new discovery of the true state of our souls. Ultimately, this childlike posture will help us to discover anew, like our brother and role-model in faith, St. Juan Diego, that we are loved, not because of some kind of imaginary perfection or cleanliness of soul, but because we are indeed the Heavenly Father's children. When we throw ourselves into His arms with childlike trust, nothing can separate us from God and His love.

I pray that those who read this thoughtful book will be led to a more profound awareness of God's love and that such love will stir up in all hearts an unbounded gratitude to our loving God, the Mighty One who "has done great things for [us], and holy is His name" (Luke 1:49).

Theodore Cardinal McCarrick

Archbishop of Washington

W hat is true of love – that without it, all other virtues and good works are valueless – is again, in another respect, true of humility. For, just as love embodies the life of all virtues and expresses the inmost substance of all holiness, humility is the *precondition* and basic presupposition for the genuineness, the beauty, and the truth of all virtue. It is *mater* and *caput* ("mother and fountainhead") of all specifically human virtues; for, inversely, pride (*superbia*) is not only by itself our primal sin, it also inwardly contaminates all intrinsically good dispositions, and robs every virtue of its value before God.

We have two great enemies to combat within us: pride and concupiscence. The two are mostly intertwined in some definite manner. Men tainted by pride alone are seldom to be met with. It is these two enemies that render us blind to value. But they are not of equal importance: it is not concupiscence but pride that constitutes the primal evil in our souls. Satan's original gesture is the act of absolute pride that rebels against God, the embodiment of all values, in an impotent attempt to appropriate His power and dominion.

True, in the sinfulness of many men (indeed, of most men) concupiscence plays a more conspicuous part; but, nevertheless, it falls short of being the primal evil. That is why in the Gospels even the sin of impurity, however grave, is less severely judged then that of pride. Christ denounced pride and obduracy in far more incisive terms than the sins of the flesh. Thus, pride is the deepest root of the malignancy within ourselves, which is entirely consonant with the fact that Adam's sin, too, consisted in the act of disobedience inspired not by concupiscence, which was only to be a consequence of the Fall, but by pride.

The fact alone that pride is the primal source of all moral evil clearly demonstrates the paramount importance of humility. What is most essential in the process of dying to ourselves is the conquest of pride and that liberation from one's self, whose name is *humility*. On the degree of our humility depends the measure in which we shall achieve freedom to participate in God's life and make it possible for the supernatural life received in holy Baptism to unfold in our souls. "God resisteth the proud and giveth grace to the humble" (James 4:6). On the other hand, every virtue and every good deed turns worthless if pride creeps into it – which happens whenever in some fashion we glory in our goodness.

Dietrich von Hildebrand
Transformation in Christ

THE LIGHT OF TRUTH

"Behold, I stand at the door and knock. If anyone hears my voice and opens the door, [then] I will enter his house and dine with him, and he with me."

REVELATION, CHAPTER 3:20

L ove does not impose itself. God, Who is Love, does not want to break into the sanctuary of a human heart. Respecting the freedom that He Himself has given us, God stands at the doors of our hearts as if He were a beggar and He knocks and waits for us to open up.

Humility does not focus on itself. Humility is completely disposed to receive and to accept God's gifts. Therefore, humility becomes openness and awaiting. A person who is humble and stands in truth discovers his own *nothingness*. As a result, this discovery evokes within him an increasing desire to be filled by the One Who is Everything. Humility opens the interior of a person to God,

Who knocks and Who wants to pour His *Everything* into small, miserable, and human *nothingness*. Humility becomes deep like an abyss with a violence that resembles a sudden draft or a gust of the wind brought forth by a vacuum that allows itself to be filled.

The opposite of humility is pride. Pride believes in itself and believes that it possesses everything in itself. It is so filled with itself that it does not need God.

God, Who knocks on the door of a human soul, is light that brings forth from the darkness the truth about a human person – the mystery of the whitewashed tomb. The Redeemer of the world knocks so that we may open the doors of our hearts to Him and allow Him to heal the wounds caused by sin.

The image of the whitewashed tomb presented herein shows the stages through which the soul can pass on its journey to God. These stages lead to the gradual rejection of the illusory image of our own *I* and to openness to the only truth that is worthy of our fascination – the Divine *You*.

The Mystery of the Whitewashed Tomb

> *"Woe to you, scribes and Pharisees, you hypocrites. You are like whitewashed tombs, which appear beautiful on the outside, but inside are full of dead men's bones and every kind of filth. Even so, on the outside you appear righteous, but inside you are filled with hypocrisy and evildoing."*
>
> Matthew, Chapter 23:27-28

In each one of us there is something of the *scribe* and the *Pharisee* who do not realize what is happening in their hearts; they do not realize the primary source of evil that is within them. The image of the exposed interior of the whitewashed tomb shows the complex relationship that takes place between a person who constantly does not know who he really is, and God, Who is knocking on the door of his heart. Gradually, stage by stage, God wants to illuminate our interior so that we, by seeing what the kingdom of our own *I* really is, will want to open up the door to Him.

CHAPTER ONE

GOD'S LIGHT THAT EXPOSES THE TRUTH ABOUT THE WHITEWASHED TOMB

During the initial stages of interior life, a person is very sure of himself. He is so convinced that he knows himself. He is so immersed in himself, so filled with an illusory faith in his own capabilities, that he does not even realize how many illusions and lies (often unconscious) are present in his self-image. Such a person feels that he is pure because he has worked hard at polishing the exterior of his own whitewashed tomb – his own *I*. He does not even believe that something is concealed underneath this polished façade, just as the whitewashed tomb conceals that which is in it. He has the impression that he is the lord of his interior kingdom and he subconsciously desires to make God one of the elements subjected to his lordship.

5

CLEANSING THE EXTERIOR OF THE TOMB

The efforts that you undertake during the initial stages of your path to holiness can be compared to cleansing the tomb's exterior. You attempt to peel off the layer of impurities that have accumulated over the years on the sepulchral surface. You scrub the tomb and you polish it. Later, you make painstaking efforts to whiten the tomb, such that one can say that the tomb looks decent.

This image of cleaning and whitening the tomb corresponds to the stage of interior life when we fight against mortal sins and eventually overcome various imperfections and weaknesses in our nature, step by step through active renunciations, sacrifices, and interior struggles. In doing this, we conquer what we can on our own before we allow God, Who knocks on the door of our dominion, to enter into it so that He Himself, by His merciful power, can realize the work of our purification.

During this stage when we are involved in cleaning the exterior of our tomb, we think that we are becoming more and more perfect. This perception corresponds to the image of perfection that is impressed on us. According to this image, reaching perfection is similar to climbing successive steps or the rungs of a ladder.

You may think, "Maybe I am climbing slowly. Nevertheless, I am ascending higher and higher." You, however, do not even know that you have fallen into a dangerous trap. **This trap is the illusion of progress that begets pride.**

It is very easy to succumb to the illusion that the successive stages of our journey to sanctity are like the progression from one grade level to another. When a child is promoted to the next grade level, he knows that a certain stage of education is now behind him, even if he critically evaluates his achievements. He will never have to repeat the curriculum of the previous level because there will be a new program in the next grade. We think of our path to holiness in a similar manner; to us, it seems that we pass from one level to the next and become more and more perfect as we go along.

THE WHITEWASHED TOMB

When the tomb is clean and white on the outside, we cling to the conviction that we are on the threshold of perfection. Since we were able to overcome many visible faults and weaknesses, we begin to think that we are almost holy and that, with just a little more effort, we will achieve sanctity.

Concerned with our own prideful plans to attain holiness by our own efforts, we fail to notice that God is knocking on the doors of our souls. We have the impression that we are almost saints. At this stage of our spiritual lives, we cannot even imagine what is hiding inside this neatly cleansed tomb.

The immense evil of our egoism is as if it were dormant and does not present any signs of activity. *In front of others, we appear to be righteous* because the events of our lives have not yet been strong enough to awaken our sleeping tendencies. Therefore, it has not even crossed our minds that *inside we are filled with hypocrisy and evildoing.*

At this stage of our interior lives, our "perfection," or rather the whitewashed appearance of our own perfection, is the source of our contentment and immense hidden pride. The sin of pride is so great that even if someone points it out directly to us we are unable to admit that we have it.

If we are able to admit to our pridefulness at this time, it is due to our human regard – our preoccupation with how others regard us. We simply believe that this is the correct thing to do.

Yet, precisely this pride causes us to be frequently critical and intolerant of others. Because we do not know how to look at our own selves in truth, we evaluate our surroundings in a subjective and biased way. When we concentrate on ourselves and on our own apparent perfection, we are open to God Who is present in our neighbor only to a very small degree. As a result, we do not hear God knocking on the doors of our souls with His light through different people and events.

Convinced of our own strength and perfection, we do not yet see how much we need God.

WHEN GOD LIFTS THE LID OF
THE WHITEWASHED TOMB

God does not want us to remain in a lie. Therefore, the moment will come when His knocking becomes stronger and more persistent. This knocking can come in the form of events that expose our interior hypocrisy and in the form of an extraordinary light of grace that shines on this interior hypocrisy. Then we are exposed to the genuine truth about ourselves. We can say that God, Who is knocking, lifts the lid of the whitewashed tomb and a luminous beam shines into its dark interior.

For the time being, the light is faint. Even this faint light, however, shows us certain fragments of the truth – the truth about ourselves in relationship to God, to ourselves, and to the world. Even though amid shadows one cannot see much, this experience is already shocking and painful.

In one's gradual discovery of the difficult truth about himself, one can see God's great gentleness and love for the soul that could otherwise become terrified and rebel. God trusts that we will not run away from this light, but rather accept it as a gift. This gift is difficult to receive, but God must give such a gift in order to rescue the beloved soul from the unconscious lie in which it is living.

When we begin to see the truth about ourselves in the Divine light, we will also begin to understand that the **perfection**, which was the source of our self-satisfaction, was **an illusion**. We removed the dirt from the *outside* of the tomb, but what we find *inside* of the tomb frequently surpasses our imagination.

The old sins that we thought we had overcome can become a real threat to us again. We see that in every moment our old sins can come back in even subtler forms.

Perhaps we will be chased again by old temptations and evil inclinations that we thought we had overcome. All of our weaknesses and sins from the past may return. Maybe we will begin to commit again the sins from which we thought we were totally free.

By discovering a small speck of the painful truth about yourself, you will surely experience the temptations of sadness, uneasiness, doubt about being loved, or even the temptation of despair. It will seem as if the firm ground on which you were standing has been removed. Maybe you will have the impression that the world in which you were living is falling apart and that the empire over which you were proudly ruling is collapsing.

This painful experience will destroy your old vision of God and your image of the journey to sanctity. It will change the way you understand the Gospel, and it will break down your former hierarchy of values, as well as your former ways of thinking.

From this point on, your awareness of your sinfulness will be much deeper than the awareness you had when you first started to whitewash the tomb. You will begin to realize that by relying on your own strength, you cannot overcome the inherent evil within you. You will see that your only rescue is to surrender your kingdom to the lordship of the One Who does not cease to knock even when you do not hear Him knocking.

During this stage on the path to holiness, it is extremely important that you want to stand in truth before

God. Your Lord desires for you to **acknowledge your own misery and simultaneously attempt to trust that He does not stop loving you** in spite of all your evil that horrifies you.

If at least a fissure appears in the armor of your distrust, then God, Who is always fighting for you, will try to take advantage of it. He will use this fissure to build an entryway into your firmly fortified world. Your egotistical reign is closed before God because you continually fear that He will diminish the reign of your *I* and that He will limit your lordship. That is why even the existence of the smallest Divine fissure is important because it can eventually be enlarged so that there will be more and more space in you for the light of Divine grace that saves you.

WHEN MORE IS EXPOSED

To the degree to which you regain spiritual equilibrium, God will be able to expose before you the next layer of fragments within the whitewashed tomb. After the first exposure, there may be a long lapse of time. However, if God wants to purify you more quickly, then He will systematically disclose more areas of your spiritual interior.

Each time more areas of your spiritual interior are exposed, you will relive the same experience as when the interior of the tomb was revealed for the first time. Now, however, the light that will enter into the tomb will turn out to be more intense. You will see not only the new fragments of the whitewashed tomb's interior, but also everything you had seen before will be revealed to you with greater clarity.

You will be convinced that you are capable of not only committing sins as you had in your past, but also worse sins.

With successive revelations of the interior of your soul, you will see that the process of graduating from one grade level to another cannot be applied to the idea of progressing toward perfection within your interior life.

Something completely different happens in interior life.

Entering a more advanced stage of interior life depends strictly on your growth in humility – a deeper lowering of yourself to make more and more space in the kingdom of your *I* for God, Who is knocking on the door. God wants to enter into this kingdom in order to forgive the infidelities you have committed as well as to preserve you from the evil that has not had the occasion to manifest itself.

As more of the whitewashed tomb is exposed, you will experience the truth about yourself more or less in a tangible way because the same temptations and sins that you had struggled with in previous stages will resurface. By seeing your interior in a clearer light, you will gradually come to discover who you really are.

You will be convinced that you are capable of committing every possible sin, to such an extent that this truth can become for you more real than everything else that surrounds you.

Perhaps you will have the impression that you are becoming worse and worse and regressing in your interior life. Perhaps you will think that you are falling down into the abyss of evil.

But do not succumb to doubt or despair – nothing bad is happening. It is only the Light that is knocking, the Light to whom you opened the borders of your kingdom. This Light is now disclosing before you the truth that your kingdom is a whitewashed tomb. It has always been a whitewashed tomb; you, however, simply did not know this before.

For the Divine Spouse Who tries hard to conquer the human heart, everything can become a means to make it so that the soul falls in love with Him without reservation. However, other people – our neighbors – fulfill special roles in this matter. This is because of their freedom that does not always submit to God's will, let alone our will!

God makes use of a difficult neighbor to gradually reveal the whitewashed tomb in us.

The light of faith is very necessary in order for us to see that the light of the Lord, Who is knocking, is hidden under the appearance of the most difficult persons around us. This neighbor alters the order that you have maintained for many years. He crucifies your plans so that at last you may begin to perceive, in the light of faith, the painful truth that you, yourself, are a difficult neighbor.

You should then be grateful not only to God but also to this neighbor who, perhaps unknowingly, is the instrument through whom God serves you, through whom He reveals the truth to you, in order to rescue and heal you.

Among the different types of evil that you will see in the whitewashed tomb, the one that will perhaps hurt you the most will be the truth that you are working **not for God's glory but for your own glory**. It will be painful for you to come to know that when you undertake different efforts and endeavors it is for yourself that you want to build a wonderful altar.

If you know that you should be giving glory to God with your work, that it should be like a prayer – a time to be in God's presence and to fulfill what He is expecting in a specific moment – then you will realize that what you do most frequently is forget about God. You will realize that what you do does not serve to adore God, but rather serves to worship yourself. After all, we cannot forget that "every virtue and every good deed turns worthless if pride creeps into it."[1]

When you carry out your own will or concentrate on yourself, you commit the sin of pride and slothfulness in the service to God, regardless of what or how much you do. It matters little even if by nature you are less active or more active.

Even if you become a missionary or build a cathedral, if you are working for your **own** glory, you are being lazy and slothful in your service **to God**.

---

[1]Dietrich von Hildebrand, *Transformation in Christ*, (New York: Longmans, Green, 1948; repr. Manchester, NH: Sophia Institute Press, 1990), 150. Originally published as *Die Umgestaltung in Christus*. Citations are to the Sophia edition.

When God shows you the pride that fills the tomb of your soul, try to accept it with the simplicity of a child. The truth is that you do everything for your own glory. However, despite this, the Heavenly Father does not stop loving you. If it is very difficult for your pride to accept this and you succumb to the temptation of sadness, try to get up right away after this fall too.

When you rise above your sadness with the simplicity of a child, God can then make your work become a real prayer. Then everything that you undertake will be done in that instance out of consideration for God and with the awareness that He is always beside you. When you forget about Him again, and when He discloses this to you again, you should get up with the simplicity of a child and begin to work with the awareness of the Lord's presence.

It would be ideal if we prayed unceasingly and constantly invited the One Who knocks into our egoistic realm. In an ideal situation, we would invite God by turning to Him in all matters, so that He could heal and cleanse us, we who are entangled in temporality. However, this is not easy. This kind of prayer is a great gift from the Lord that only those who are humble and children of the Gospel receive.

God surely will bestow this grace upon you also. However, this will happen when, by getting to know the interior of the whitewashed tomb in a clearer and clearer light, you begin to understand more deeply how great His love is for you. How great is the love of the One Who unceasingly knocks at your door, even though He knows the entire truth about your life: its dirt and misery.

Your astonishment will be wonderful when you see that **He is not disgusted by your uncleanliness.** You are the one who is so ashamed of your dirt, and you are the one whom He embraces with His love saying, "Do not worry, I love you just as you are and I will purify you with great tenderness."

THE WHITEWASHED TOMB BEFORE THE EYES OF OTHERS

When you continue your discovery of the truth about the ugliness of your soul's interior, you will gradually begin to understand that any trust placed in you by others is simply a miracle of God's mercy.

You owe the fact that others see only the exterior of your whitewashed tomb, and perhaps even admire you, to God's grace.

In a certain way, this is God's special intervention due to His grace so that you can more thoroughly discover the filth that dominates your tomb's interior and simultaneously attract others closer to Christ with your exterior greatness.

You then become like a prop that God uses as His instrument.

It is best if you do not forget that God Himself remains in control of the situation. Since He performs the miracle that the truth about you remains hidden from the eyes of others, then He can also disclose it at any moment.

If you had the posture of an evangelical child, then you would not be excessively preoccupied about the possibility that God can reveal your true self to anybody. You would leave this entire matter in God's hands. After all, He is the One Who decides everything.

When others praise you or even admire you, you can say to the Lord:

> *I know that the truth about me is what I see in the interior of the whitewashed tomb. If this is hidden from others, it is only because You want it this way. Thank You for using my miserable nature. I desire to be Your servant in everything.*

You do not have to analyze this too much. Do not be distracted by this truth. After all, the Master may desire to dress His servant magnificently and to seat him at a place of honor at the table. As a result, someone may consider this servant to be a very important guest. However, in such a situation, the servant would be ridiculous to take over this adopted role as if it were real. It is best if the servant remembers who he really is.

Your Lord expects you to be grateful for the gifts with which He unceasingly showers you. Thank Him for the grace of exposing the interior of the whitewashed tomb. Thank

Him also for hiding from the eyes of others what only you can see. Thank Him for using you – a whitewashed tomb – as an instrument for His holy plans. If it is His will, however, that the truth about you is revealed to others, then you should also accept this, with gratitude.

CHAPTER TWO

SO THAT THE TRUTH DOES NOT TERRIFY YOU

E xposing the interior of the tomb is an unceasing process in spiritual life, especially during the period of purifications. God, by knocking on the door of your soul, expects you to entrust to Him the mystery of the whitewashed tomb. He expects that you will not hide the truth about yourself under the mask of the Pharisee. Do not be afraid of this Light that is knocking. This Light is showing you the sick parts of your soul in order to heal them. When you discover how seriously ill you are, you should then trustfully surrender these dark parts of your soul to the healing Light. To your great surprise, you will be convinced that, although the discovery of the filth of the whitewashed tomb is painful, it is a great gift from God.

For example, look at the prodigal son. The long road that led away from the father's house was a course on which the prodigal son not only saw, but also experienced the truth about his misery. As he discovered more and more of his misery, he eventually was unable to handle the truth by himself and began his return home. Somehow, he must have surmised that there, somewhere at home, the light of his father's goodness was waiting for him – that there he would find his rescue.

FOLLOWING THE PRODIGAL SON'S EXAMPLE

Looking at the prodigal son's drama, you may perceive yourself in it.

When you see your soul's interior in full light, you may feel similar to the prodigal son after he squandered his father's fortune. The son dreamt about eating the husks from the pigs' trough. He found himself in a situation worse than the swine to which he was tending because no one even offered him the food that the pigs ate. He had reached the bottom of his human misery, the lowest humiliation.

Nevertheless, you should not forget what the prodigal son did next or the kind of decision that he made. In response to this situation, the son decided: "I shall get up and go to my father" (Lk 15:18). God wants you to repeat these words every time that you are standing at the edge of the whitewashed tomb experiencing the bitterness connected to seeing your own misery. Each painful discovery of the whitewashed tomb should lead you to decide to return to the Father.

Remember that the Father does not stop waiting for you, not even for a moment.

The Father is unceasingly knocking on your door. He is knocking not only with the truth about the whitewashed tomb of your soul, but also with His mercy, ready to pour it over your misery at every moment.

However, you should not forget that a battle will be waged for your soul. Your reason, unenlightened by faith, as well as your experience and feelings, might question your decision to return to the Father.

Reason unenlightened by faith will present to you the new images of misery, which were revealed with subsequent exposures of the interior of the whitewashed tomb. It will tell you that it is impossible for God to love someone like you. Reason will tell you that even if this love were possible, you do not have a right to it.

Experience can suggest to you that, in the past, God always received you with love; however, the gravity of your evil is greater now. So now what? You may question whether or not the Father will still receive you. You may begin to feel disgusted with yourself and your impression that evil fills you to the brim.

Also, your **feelings** will not help you to trust in God's love. These feelings will inhibit you from being open to Him Who unceasingly knocks at the door. The sadness, discouragement and doubts that flood you at the sight of your own misery are, after all, very bad advisors.

These negative feelings are generated by the pride that does not want to accept the misery that you have discovered. To accept your misery is only possible if something of the posture of a child who tries to open himself up to God's grace emerges within you. Only by assuming such a posture, will you see the glimmer of light that indicates where your rescue is.

EXPOSING THE WHITEWASHED TOMB'S INTERIOR BEFORE ONE'S CONFESSOR

If you become childlike, it will be easier for you to open up to the Divine truth's light, which knocks on your door and reaches out to you through your confessor. You would be unwise to allow your human regard for what the priest may think about you to prevent you from telling him what the recent discoveries within the whitewashed tomb have allowed you to see in yourself. It would be best if, with the simplicity and openness of a child, you told him about all of the newly discovered layers of misery that God has shown you by illumining your soul's interior with His light.

Try not to look at your confessor merely in human terms.

If you have a childlike posture, it will be easier for you to see Christ in your confessor, knocking on the door of your soul. You should look at Christ, not at the instrument that He is using.

After all, your Redeemer knows very well what is hidden in the interior of the whitewashed tomb. He desires for you to simply tell Him about the concrete symptoms of your evil.

Are you afraid of disappointing your confessor by fully acknowledging before him the truth about who you are?

This is because of pride and human regard. Christ, with Whom you meet during confession, has been patiently waiting for you to tell the truth. By knocking on your door, He asks you to confess that truth.

God desires you to be like a child who first throws himself into his father's arms and later thinks about his own unworthiness. It is best to first confess your entire misery to Christ, Who is hidden in the priest, and then later – together with your Savior – analyze and reflect on your situation.

THE EXPOSED INTERIOR OF THE WHITEWASHED TOMB IN MOSES' LIFE

What can help you to courageously accept the successive discoveries of what lies within the whitewashed tomb is the awareness that great figures in the history of Salvation might have gone through similar experiences.

For example, you can look at Moses' forty-year journey, during which time he led the Chosen People to the Promised Land. It must have been painful for him to witness the Israelites' unceasing rebelliousness. Perhaps he experienced these as consecutive discoveries of his whitewashed tomb. After all, while he was leading the Chosen People because of God's will, he was feeling responsible for forming in them a proper posture toward the Lord. Meanwhile, for forty years, Moses witnessed their successive rebelliousness. He saw how the people entrusted to him continuously did not understand the ways of the

Lord, and how they turned away from these ways. Through different situations and events throughout the pilgrimage across the desert, Moses saw that the Israelites were constantly blind and deaf to God's knocking.

The Israelites constantly forgot about the miracles that God had performed for them, as well as the truths that God had shown them through Moses. This lack of progress and constant defiance must have been a crushing experience for Moses. It is reminiscent of the effort of Sisyphus,[2] who unceasingly had to see how the stone that he had to roll up a hill, with great effort, rolled back down again and again.

This can be compared to the experience of parents who suffer failure when raising children. Does education not resemble the work of Sisyphus? Parents can feel as if they have wasted their entire lives when despite their years of effort in trying to instill proper principles in their children and guide their children to God, their children turn away from God and do not live according to these principles.

After many years of painful experiences, how did God Himself assess Moses?

On that very day the LORD said to Moses, "Go up on Mount Nebo, here in the Abarim Mountains [it is in the land of Moab facing

---

[2] "Sisyphus – in Greek mythology was a man condemned to the unending punishment of rolling a heavy stone up a hill. Each time he got the stone to the top, it plunged down, and he had to begin again. Sisyphus, a king of Corinth ... angered Zeus. When Sisyphus died, Hades kept the trickster eternally busy rolling his stone." *Encyclopedia Americana*, 2000 ed., s.v. "Sisyphus."

Jericho], and view the land of Canaan, which I am giving to the Israelites as their possession. Then you shall die on the mountain you have climbed, and shall be taken to your people, just as your brother Aaron died on Mount Hor and there was taken to his people; because both of you broke faith with me among the Israelites at the waters of Meribath-kadesh in the desert of Zin by failing to manifest my sanctity among the Israelites. You may indeed view the land at a distance, but you shall not enter that land which I am giving to the Israelites" (Deut 32:48-52).

This was God's own assessment, so Moses could not doubt that it was just. After the series of failures and setbacks which Moses experienced in guiding the Chosen People, as well as their hurtful rebelliousness, God evaluated His servant very precisely. Could Moses have had any doubts regarding his uselessness as a servant who did not fulfill the task given to him? Could he have doubted that his failure was the reason why he did not enter the Promised Land? The Lord told Moses that he would die even though Moses was still strong and humanly able to lead God's people. However, despite Moses' strength, God's will was different (see Deut 34:7).

God revealed Moses' misery to him; He clearly revealed to Moses that he would not lead the Israelites into the land of Canaan because of his unfaithfulness. The explicit discovery – "look, you were unfaithful and a useless servant" – was, as if, the last exposure of what was inside the interior of Moses' whitewashed tomb. We may say that Moses had good reason to feel rejected by God. However, we can only imagine how surprised Moses must have been when, after his death, because of God's mercy, he entered the spiritual Promised Land, where he would abide for all eternity. The example of Moses shows us that on the road to sanctity, God has the right to completely strip a person and crush him with the sight of his misery. God's light can reveal to someone that he achieves no success of his own. If this person hears the knocking of the merciful Lord in these dramatic events and trustfully opens his door to Jesus, then he will also experience what Jesus Christ foretold: "I will enter his house and dine with him, and he with me" (Rev 3:20).

Not everyone has to go through experiences as difficult as those of Moses and of other great saints. You may have only a few trials in your own life and you may find, to your great surprise, that God will bestow upon you the gift of holiness at the moment of your death. You may see that, in response to giving over all of your misery to Him with childlike trust, God will show you His boundless mercy and lead you into His Kingdom. Then, you will meet face to face with the One Who knocked each day through internal and external events on the borders of your egoistic country so that you would open the door and let Him in. In opening the door to Christ, you allow Him to transform your egoistic country into God's Kingdom, a spiritual Promised Land.

BEING CARRIED IN THE BLESSED MOTHER'S ARMS OVER THE ABYSS OF ONE'S OWN EVIL

When your soul becomes despondent upon seeing your evil, try to remember that, because of the desire that Christ expressed as He was dying on the Cross, you are Mary's beloved child and you are being carried in Her arms (see Jn 19:25-27). For those who follow the way of consecration to Mary according to the example of St. John the Apostle,[3] remembering Christ's last testament given from the Cross can be very helpful in difficult moments, especially in those moments when they discover the truth about who they really are. If you are traveling on this road and hovering over the abyss of the exposed interior of your whitewashed tomb, which is filled with filth, trust that **Mary never lets go of you**

---

[3] Consecration to Mary according to the example of St. John the Apostle contains the principle elements of the spirituality of living in communion of life with Christ through Mary. The desire to strive toward holiness is also the desire to build one's spiritual life on the foundation of humility so that one's life may bear full fruit. In the formation of the virtue of humility, it is important to be conscious of one's spiritual misery while maintaining the firm conviction of one's particular dignity as a child of God and as a sinner who was redeemed by Jesus and filially adopted by the power of His Redemptive Sacrifice. Humility, as the simultaneous acknowledgment of one's own misery and one's own dignity as God's child, opens one up in a special way to the mystery of the Redemptive Sacrifice.

The deepening of the perception of one's spiritual misery is a process that lasts throughout one's entire life. This process requires, among other things, renunciation of illusions about one's self. This means to continually see one's self in truth in order to see what one is really like. In other words, this means to see one's self in God's eyes. It is not at all easy to see one's self as God does because God perceives the individual as His beloved child. At the same time, God also sees the individual's wretchedness and sins, which were the cause of the passion and death of Jesus Christ.

It is necessary to admit the truth about one's evil that crucified Jesus Christ; however, this acknowledgment must be accompanied by a deep conviction that, through the power of Christ's perfect sacrifice, one is already redeemed. The more one comes to know his own misery, the more he needs to be convinced that

and always holds you in Her loving arms. This will prevent you from falling into the abyss.

If you see your spiritual misery with faith in God's love, then this truth will not threaten you. If, however, you start to doubt God's mercy, then newly discovered misery could lead you even to despair. Doubting God's mercy could provoke you to close the door of your heart before Him, thus directing you to commit even worse sins. But if you try to remember that you are being carried in the arms of Mary, the Mother of Christ, you will be fully open to God's love. In Her

---

he is God's beloved child. Otherwise, he will not be able to humbly accept his own evil.

Only those who, losing their illusions about themselves, reach out their hands trustfully toward the Father and await everything from Him attain this posture. For some, however, it may be very difficult to rely directly on the mercy of God. Thus, those who find it difficult to open up directly to God's mercy are given the opportunity to seek aid in Mary, since Christ gave Her to all individuals as their mother and made Her the Mother of the Church. Christ entrusted each individual to Mary, just as He entrusted St. John the Apostle to Mary through His testament uttered from the Cross. By the power of these words, just like St. John the Apostle, every individual has the right to live in communion with the Mother of the Church, and to seek in this union a greater and deeper chance for union with God.

On the path to sanctity, one begins to notice his nothingness in various aspects of his spiritual life. This manifests itself, among other things, by the fact that it is very difficult for one to acknowledge one's nothingness while simultaneously maintaining the firm conviction that one is loved as a child of God. Due to this difficulty, the path of St. John the Apostle through communion of life with Mary is a chance because it allows one to uncover God's mercy all the more fully. This path becomes an opportunity for one to live in the image and likeness of Jesus Christ, through the communion of life with Mary, in order to finally obey His will to the point of accepting even death. If one wants to build this obedience on the foundation of humility, then it is best brought about when one does not give himself credit for God's graces. Thus Christ, Who stoops down over one's misery, gives us Mary and, through Her, shows us His mercy. Therefore, one is entrusted to the Mother of the Church, and Christ allows one to invite Her into one's heart, so that She will live the Gospel in one and for one. She will form the complete image of Her Son in the individual's soul, so that it will no longer be the individual who lives, but Christ living in the individual, for the individual, and through the individual (cf. Gal 2:20).

arms, you may be shielded from your faults and unfaithfulness; you may experience peacefulness and even happiness when God reveals the contents of your whitewashed tomb to you in a fuller light. This is exactly what happened in the lives of the saints. They saw to a large degree the truth about themselves. They were quite convinced that they were capable of committing every kind of sin, and they vividly discovered various degrees of their own unfaithfulness. Their boundless trust in God's mercy, however, prevented them from committing the sins that they saw in their whitewashed tombs.

THE FINAL EXPOSURE AT THE MOMENT OF DEATH

When God decides to completely remove the lid of the whitewashed tomb, you will clearly see what is inside. No detail of your misery will escape your notice. At the same time, you will have nowhere to run in order to escape this sight. This will be the most painful exposure. You may feel like you are the worst person in the world, and you may experience temptations against faith, or doubts regarding God's mercy. At the moment of your death, this last exposure may resemble a freefall into the abyss of misery. You will have to make your final decision: you may willingly choose evil and be immersed in it for all of eternity, or you may believe that, despite this misery that fills your soul, God loves you. By accepting this truth, you open yourself up to the grace of redemption. The Lord may want you to be like Moses; He may will that you die with the deep conviction that you are an ineffective servant **who cannot count on any of his merits, but rather, only on God's mercy.**

Perhaps this kind of experience happens to all of the saints. It is possible that at the moment of death, they fully discover the content of the whitewashed tomb of their souls.[4] If a saint receives this experience as a form of God's knocking, then a saint will hear the Savior's voice and will open the door. Then, with profound trust, a saint will stand before God, acknowledging his own misery, fully aware that he does not deserve salvation because of his unfaithfulness. Then Jesus Christ will immerse this saint in His Redemptive Sacrifice and will save him by His own love.

This kind of discovery of the whitewashed tomb is possible only because of faith. The Divine light of truth desires to illuminate the inner part of your heart so you can discover that the whitewashed tomb, which you consider beautiful and worthy of notice, is really filled with misery. Consecutive disclosures of the whitewashed tomb are supposed to convince you that your only rescue is to open the door of your heart and give yourself over to the Redeemer – to the One Who is knocking. This happened in the life of St. Faustina Kowalska.

"Jesus said to me, **'My daughter, you have not offered Me that which is really yours. . . . Daughter, give Me**

---

[4] Blessed Pier Giorgio Frassati, who was an extraordinary joyful person during his life, when making the sign of the Cross a few moments before his death, full of fear, he said in a worried whisper: "Will the good God forgive me?" and then exclaimed: "Pardon me, Lord!" Robert Claude, *The Soul of Pier-Giorgio Frassati*, trans. Una Morrisy, (New York: Spiritual Book Assoc., 1960), 117.

your misery, because it is your exclusive property.'"[5] In the life of St. Faustina Kowalska, the Lord Jesus loved her desire to lower herself, her desire to live in truth, and her desire to be humble. Humility becomes a beautiful opening to and awaiting for God, especially when, discovering the truth, one is unable to concentrate on himself and adore his own ego. After all, is the filth of your whitewashed tomb worthy of such attention? The filth inside the whitewashed tomb is an insignificant, tiny, miserable nothing, undeserving of your admiration or even notice. Humility is the truth that opens you to God Who knocks on your door. Without humility, He would be unable to unite Himself with a soul that is so preoccupied with itself by adoring the illusory ego. Humility becomes openness and awaiting for God when a person ceases to believe in his own greatness – when he ceases to trust in himself. Then and only then will a person begin to believe not in himself but in the greatness of God. A humble person places all of his hope in God.

God falls in love with the posture of humility precisely because He can pour out the ocean of His mercy into the humble spirit.

---

[5] Maria Faustina Kowalska, *Diary: Divine Mercy in My Soul,* 3rd. ed. Rev. (Stockbridge, MA: Marians of the Immaculate Conception, 2003), notebook 4, no. 1318.

The Mystery of the Human Heart that Relies on God

God gave you freedom and it is precisely because of this extraordinary gift that you can love God. Love cannot exist without freedom. We cannot force anyone to love. This is why the prodigal son's father agreed to let his son leave and rebel.

Our Lord loves human freedom; it is His wonderful gift, thanks to which we can respond to His love. Being endowed with the gift of freedom entails the risk that we will use this gift against the Lord Himself. The mystery of man's openness to God's love lies in freedom. But in this same freedom there is a puzzling evil – a human heart's secret and murky realm that does not want to respond to the Lord's knocking.

Why some hearts take advantage of the gift of freedom in order to receive God's love and why others use this gift against the Love of the One Who is knocking will remain a hidden mystery for us. The question pertains not so much to the mystery of human evil that lies in the depths of the soul, but rather to what lies at the root of this evil. It is not easy to discover or trace this evil because it hides under "innocent" disguises. The moment will inevitably come, however, when God will want to point out that the very root of your own evil is pride. Pride causes you to be self-assured and self-sufficient; it is precisely pride that closes you to the light of God's truth.

In order to rescue you, God will reveal to you that pride is the root of all the filth and worms found inside your soul, the very soul on whose door He is knocking. In the light of God's grace, you will see how the wonderful gifts that you have continually received for free from God have been destroyed in the sea of your pride.

CHAPTER THREE

THE DEAD SEA AND THE ROCKY EDIFICE OF PRIDE

I n the human soul there is always an intermingling of two opposing realities. One is the richness of the presence of God's grace and the other is the destructive poison of pride. Pride is not only a sin in itself, but also a poison that spreads and contaminates every good thing that is in us. When pride creeps into them, every good deed and virtue become tainted and deprived of their own value.[6]

Our pride, which concentrates so much on itself, does not even hear the Lord's strong knocking. It is like hard stone – impenetrable to God's love that is trying to rescue us. Therefore, this Light, which knocks on the door of our soul in order to heal it, must first expose the truth about our closed, lifeless, inner self that is full of pride.

---

[6] Cf. von Hildebrand, *Transformation in Christ*, 150.

THE SYMBOLIC MEANING OF THE DEAD SEA

The Dead Sea is a vast body of water that contains no life. The salt concentration of the Dead Sea is four times greater than other oceans. The concentration of salt is so high that no life can exist. A depressing and cemetery-like atmosphere pervades the Dead Sea, and the lifeless hills that surround it only add to the somber mood.

Does not a human soul permeated with pride resemble the lifeless waters of the Dead Sea? Does not pride oppose God's life-giving graces, which He constantly bestows upon the soul, just like salt prevents life in the Dead Sea? Despite what you would probably think, the Dead Sea is not an entirely closed receptacle. Pure water from the River Jordan flows into the Dead Sea, bringing it an entire richness of life. Over 6.5 million tons of life-giving water flow into the sea every day after passing through the fertile fish-filled Beginatha Lake. However, all of that rich life perishes in its salty depths and disappears without a trace. The evaporation there is so strong that neither the level of water nor the level of saltiness undergoes any change.

It does not take much for us to compare the life-giving waters of the Jordan River to the deluge of God's grace, which we unceasingly experience because He knocks on the doors of our hearts in every moment of our lives. Continually, new waves of God's grace come to us during prayer and especially during the Divine Sacrifice of the Eucharist. We must remember that somewhere in the world the words of consecration are being uttered and the Redemptive Sacrifice of Jesus Christ is being offered at practically every moment. Because there are approximately 400,000 priests spread out on all the continents, we can assume that at every moment somewhere in the world the Eucharist is being celebrated. As a result, the entire world is constantly being immersed in the Divine Sacrifice and flooded with an infinite number of graces. At the same time, the opposition of human hearts to God's grace must be great because this deluge of graces has not transformed us, given us life, or deepened our interior lives.

Is it not pride, then, which kills all signs of supernatural life within the soul? Is not this pride like the Dead Sea's contaminated and poisonous water that kills every living organism that flows into it? We call ourselves Christians and yet we live as if God does not exist. The lifeless sea of our pride and our disordered self-love destroy countless graces that flow to us from God. These graces are wasted because we are closed to them. This often occurs because we lack the patience of awaiting Christ in the Eucharist, in our prayer lives, and in our meetings with others. All of the desires that close our hearts to Jesus Christ, Who is knocking on our doors, are contained within this contaminated sea of pride. Our desire to have a good, easy, comfortable life leads to a lack of radicalism in our service to God. God loves us and He does not agree to this. The Light Who is knocking on the doors of our souls will point out to us how these desires are illusions that close us to God's action within us. If this is not enough, then God will have to burn everything that can destroy us in order to rescue us.

CALLING FOR THE LIFE-GIVING FLOOD

When you discover the truth about yourself it is very important to simultaneously invoke in yourself an act of trust, to the point of folly, in God's mercy. When you see how closed you are to God's graces, you can imitate St. Thérèse of the Child Jesus. When she discovered the truth about herself, she would say that remaining a little child before God is "to recognize our nothingness, to [await] everything from God . . . ."[7] In the humble acknowledgement of your own misery, with boundless trust, await an even greater flood of graces from God, praying:

> Lord, I believe that You love me because You do not cease to knock on the door of my heart. You continually give me new graces even though I waste the ones that I receive. I acknowledge my own spiritual misery, which closely resembles the image of the Dead Sea. But, I await everything from You. I extend my hands toward You and await the flood of Your graces that will enliven the dead sea of my soul so that I can witness the miracle of my heart's openness to Your graces.

---

[7] Thérèse of Lisieux, St. Thérèse of Lisieux: Her Last Conversations, trans. John Clarke, (Washington, DC: ICS Publications, 1977), 138. Translation of J'ENTRE DANS LA VIE, Derniers Entretiens (Editions du Cerf – Desclée de Brouwer, 1973). Citation is from the "Yellow Notebook" of Mother Agnes, entry from August 6, 1897. – Ed.

Repeat this as often as possible, regardless of whether or not the Divine light of truth reveals your pride to you or hides it from you. The most important thing is that you try to see it with the eyes of faith.

At various spiritual stages you can always acknowledge that you are like the Dead Sea of pride and, by your faith, you can call upon the abyss of God's mercy. You can take up this posture not only during the celebration of the Holy Eucharist, adoration of the Blessed Sacrament, and meditation, but also during short ejaculatory prayers during the day. If you acknowledge in the light of faith that you are like the Dead Sea, and yet you continue to call upon God's mercy, then, through the eyes of faith, you will also see the flood of graces that will be poured over you.

THE ACCUMULATING EDIFICE OF PRIDE

As much as the Dead Sea symbolizes the destructive and contaminated influence of pride, pride's hardness and resistance to change can also be compared to a massive rock. "Pride determines a specifically grave form of obduracy," writes Dietrich von Hildebrand.[8] This massive rock formation of pride not only continually opposes God's grace, but also continually increases in size. Even very insignificant achievements in any area of your life can inflate your pride: financial, educational, domestic, professional, or spiritual. Our **reaction to success** is a good measuring stick for what

---

[8] Von Hildebrand, *Transformation in Christ*, 153.

really happens in our souls. Often just a crumb of sympathy, a little praise, an inflow of extra money, or a task carried out properly will be a source of egotistical joy and will feed our pride. Pride is not picky and, with the exception of true humility, it can feed off of just about everything. When considering this truth, one may ask, "Is it worthwhile to make any effort in order to achieve anything in one's life? If any success or achievement, such as an advancement or earning a doctorate degree for example, can contribute to the regression of our interior lives, then perhaps we should not consider bettering ourselves in an external way?" If what we want to do is not connected to God's will, then indeed we should not pursue it because doing anything against the One Who is the Lord of the world is utter stupidity.

God can reveal to us when He wants us to achieve a higher position in the eyes of society. In addition, He will reveal what we are obligated to do in any new position. But even fulfilling God's will, when it is connected to some kind of achievement or success, can increase our pride. Because of this, it is important to lower ourselves in our own eyes and remember that our souls resemble the lifeless waters of the Dead Sea and that we cannot attribute any of our successes to ourselves.

CAN YOU CRUSH A MASSIVE ROCK WITH A PICK AX?

Each success should trigger an alarm in your heart, calling you to undertake an ever increasing effort to be humble. This is very similar to striking a massive edifice with a pick ax; although you become very tired from exerting a lot of effort and making a lot of noise, the result is minute.

After hours of hard work there will be but a few chips of stone carved from the massive rock you are attacking. Even after many years of exerting hard labor by beating against your own pride, you will only be able to crush a tiny little piece of the rock at its base. No one with any bit of common sense would assume that a person equipped with a pick ax could crush Mount Everest. At the same time, the edifice that you want to destroy constantly grows. In reality, you will not even be able to break off that which just grew out of it.

It is true that by a very conscientious effort to fight for humility you might diminish the massive formation of your pride in a very limited way. When God notices that you are not succumbing to quietism[9] or giving into discouragement, then He Himself can grind the edifice to dust. Therefore the pick ax of active renunciation should

---

[9] Quietism is a "general name for any view of the spiritual life that minimizes human activity and moral responsibility. But more properly it refers to the theories of Miguel de Molinos (c. 1640-97) and François Fénelon (1651-1715), Archbishop of Cambrai. Its basic position is that, to become perfect, one must be totally passive, annihilate one's will and so totally abandon oneself to God that one cares for neither heaven nor hell. In prayer, the perfect soul makes no acts of love or petition, or even of adoration. Such total passivity makes mortification or the sacraments useless. Sin becomes impossible to perfect souls. Quietism was condemned in the person of Molinos by Pope Innocent XI in 1687, and Fénelon by Innocent XII in 1691." *Modern Catholic Dictionary*, (1999) s.v. "Quietism."

always be in your hands.[10] This is especially important when, by God's will, you either hold an important position or have been assigned an important task because these human accomplishments can cause your pride to violently swell, thus increasing your resistance to God's graces.

God does not want you to look at this idly.

Not only power, but also knowledge can constitute a very corruptive element. When you know something, you have an advantage over those who do not have that knowledge. In some situations knowledge can even be a source of power. This can give birth to feelings of superiority or a desire to show off to others. The One Who humbled Himself until He died on the Cross encourages us, regardless of the stage of our interior lives, to always undertake new ways to crush the massive rock that symbolizes our pride of power, knowledge, or self-assurance.

The important thing is not to become discouraged. If you get discouraged then you will resemble a child who tries to destroy a mountain with a pick ax. But, seeing how little progress he makes after a few attempts, he despondently looks at his father and sadly puts away the tool. When it

---

[10] In the light of St. John of the Cross' doctrine, one can differentiate an active and a passive aspect of a human soul's purifications. In active purifications, the soul takes the initiative when it comes to the mortification of his concupiscence and desires, whereas during passive purifications, the accent goes more to the side of God's action. Man's participation then is more passive, disposed and willing to receive the Divine purifications. Both aspects of purification – active and passive – compliment each other. In the spiritual pilgrimage toward God, it is not enough to submit oneself to the purifying action. God expects a soul to be disposed for it, and to make active renunciations by its own initiative.

becomes difficult for you, try to remember that **those efforts,** although not very externally effective, **are very pleasing to God.** Perhaps the Lord will receive them as an invitation to enter through the door upon which He knocks. In this way, your meager efforts will allow God to enter into your life with His grace because, after all, only the power of that grace can grind to dust the massive rock formation of your pride.

WHEN GOD INTERVENES WITH HIS GRACE

By our own efforts we can never earn God's grace. It is a gift freely given from Him. Nevertheless, we should always beg for it. In our fight against pride, active renunciations are like the trusting pleas of a child who says:

> *Daddy, You know that the work You entrusted to me is beyond my capacity. But I want to do everything that is in my power and, because of this desire, I am not discouraged. I know that You desire my efforts and that You will not refuse me Your grace. I trust that it is You Yourself Who crushes my pride. I know that You will overcome my resistance in the face of Your love.*

Can the loving Father refuse anything to the child who places his trust in Him? Jesus responds to that question, "What father among you would hand his son a snake when he asks for a fish? Or hand him a scorpion when he asks for an egg? If you then, who are wicked, know how to give good gifts to your children, how much more will the Father in heaven give the holy Spirit to those who ask him?" (Lk 11:11-13).

God desires to strengthen your perseverance, which is born of the foundation of your childlike trust. If He allows you to undergo trials, He does so not in order that you give up or become discouraged in your endeavors to overcome the obstacles that lay before you. Rather, you undergo trials of faith so that **you may acknowledge your own weaknesses and more zealously call upon God's might** while, at the same time, practicing humility. If you gave up your active renunciations, claiming that you are incapable of destroying the massive edifice of pride by your own strength with a little pick ax, then this would be false humility. Every falsehood especially wounds God Who loves the truth. He wants you to grow in authentic humility and fight against any discouragement.

Even if you are unable to see any fruits from your efforts until death, you should not give up practicing active renunciations.[11] God Who is knocking on the door of your heart can intervene with His grace even at the very last moment of your life. You must trust Him without reservation. On the other hand, if, despite your attempts to open the door of your soul, the Lord still does not intercede with His cleansing power and He does not seem to intervene,

---

[11] St. Thérèse of Lisieux describes her soul up until the age of fourteen: "My soul was like a beautiful tree, whose blossoms had scarcely opened when they fell . . . If God wills you also to have this experience, then offer up the sacrifice to Him: in other words, . . . If He permits all the flowers of your holy desires and good will to fall to the ground without any fruit, do not worry." Sister Geneviève of the Holy Face (Céline Martin), A Memoir of My Sister, St. Thérèse, trans. Carmelite Sisters of New York (New York: P.J. Kenedy & Sons, 1959), 37-38. Authorized translation of Conseils et Souvenirs. – Ed.

then you should also be grateful for this. Perhaps He constantly has to hide from you because of your soul's resistant state. It is the best situation if you do not know if you are being purified or not.

A person who sees his resistance to God's action more clearly, especially when God's grace discloses the profound discrepancy between the actual state of his soul and the Lord's expectations, while simultaneously recognizing the richness of grace that God offers him, may conclude that he is regressing in his spiritual life. Even if a person thought that he was entering a more advanced phase of his interior life in the past, when he sees how he wastes the river of graces that God offers him now, the only thing that he can do is to fully trust in God's infinite mercy.

WHY ARE YOU STILL ALIVE?

The realization that you are a dead sea of pride should increase your inner awareness and the conviction that you waste more and more of God's graces. In order to prevent you from wasting His gifts, God can take your very life away from you. Should the One Who loves you idly stand by and watch as you constantly trample upon all of the graces that He gives you? God knows that it would be better if He took your life at the most advantageous moment for your soul rather than allowing you to choose a prolonged stay in purgatory. If you want to live in truth, then you should live with the awareness that you may die at any moment. The fact that you are still alive is an expression of God's mercy, but if you died, that too would be a sign of His mercy.

Life in the face of death should be accompanied not only by the fear that you can die as a result of natural causes, but above all else, life in the face of death should be permeated with the consciousness that your death can occur at any moment because God takes into consideration the state of your soul. After all, whether you die now or die later depends totally on God. Any effort on your part to preserve your life, either by living cautiously or taking the best medicine, is futile if God decides, in His mercy, that it is better for your soul if your body is dead.

The moment of your death depends primarily on your soul's disposition. If you are wasting more and more graces, then God, in order to preserve you from wasting more graces, can take away your life.

Under these conditions, what can you do so as not to become discouraged? You have to trust that God is infinitely merciful. Without ceasing to consider that you deserve to die like the Good Thief, do not become discouraged. God desires that, while practicing active renunciations, you await His intervention in your life. If you are still alive, then it means that God has plans for you and awaits your conversion with hope. He awaits your greater perseverance to strike the massive fortress of your pride with the pick ax of active renunciations. He desires that you will hand yourself over to Him in every aspect of your life and await everything from His merciful love.

CHAPTER FOUR

THE POND OF PRIDE OF HUMAN REGARD

One kind of pride that the light of God's truth excavates from the murky parts of your whitewashed tomb is the pride of human regard. Pride contains a lethal poison that consists of changing images. In other words, as the center of his world, man replaces the image of God that is placed in his soul through the act of creation itself, with his own egotistical *I*. This is the phenomenon of spiritual narcissism. Thirsty after long hours of hunting, the Narcissus of mythology stooped down over a little pond and he saw on the water's surface the reflection of his face, which expressed all of his yearnings and desires. Enchanted by what he saw, he could not tear himself away from looking at his own reflection. In the end, he died because of his love for his own reflection.

Other kinds of pride are always connected to some form of satisfying our human needs and exteriorly directed lusts. Narcissistic pride, which has many degrees and shades, singularly strives to concentrate on one's own *I* by subordinating everything else to its desire for its own supremacy, power, and praise. The exterior world becomes as if engulfed by and caught up in the contemporary narcissist's desire for and delight in the feeling of his own importance. The narcissist not only adores himself, but also awaits acceptance, confirmation of his own self-worth, and even adoration by others.

The mythical example of Narcissus presents a kind of warning. Perhaps you, too, are in love with yourself? Are you not led in your endeavors only by what you consider to be important? You are peering into the pond of the pride of human regard and you see illusory images – yourself, your life, and your own vision of the world. You are so absorbed by these visions that it is as if the real world has stopped to exist for you. The One Who constantly knocks on the door of your heart is Truth Who wants to rescue you.

THE GOSPEL ACCORDING TO NARCISSUS

Narcissus is perversely in love with himself. Although unconsciously, he inhibits the action of grace by creating **his own vision** of self and the world, his own images of God and His will, and his own personal version of God's teachings. We can say that he often unconsciously dares to use a gospel oriented toward his own advantage, a gospel that has very little in common with the text inspired by the Holy Spirit. Narcissus gazes at his own image with admiration and thinks that God Himself must be like him. Therefore, he interprets the Gospel according to his own convictions, seeking in the Word of God **statements that justify his way of life.** In this way he closes his heart toward this "knocking" Light and is not at all interested in what God really wants to tell him.

Do you not have within yourself something of the narcissist? Perhaps you convince yourself that you are either undertaking or giving up some endeavors because of God's will. In every moment, in order for you to see what God truly expects from you, you have to take your eyes off your own image and fix them on the Lord. If you still concentrate on yourself, then even though you say that you search for God's will, you essentially do what you yourself consider right and in agreement with the vision reflected on the surface of your own pond. God's light of truth wants to disclose before you the real, unconscious motives that direct your life, your daily choices, and your actions.

Even if, without any objection, you acknowledge that you are far from perfect, this does not mean that you are not in love with yourself. Perhaps, once in a while, you can be awakened from this state, for example, during confession. If the words of your confessor disturb you, then they can pull you away from this preoccupation with yourself. The words do not mean much, however, when you quickly return to contemplating your own reflection. You change the truth that Jesus wants to reveal to you through His confessor so that this disturbing message will fit your own expectations and stop bruising your own ego.

Upon seeing your closed-mindedness toward God's will, an experienced priest will try to explain everything precisely, so that you will have no doubts about these matters. Unfortunately, if you lack good will, then even the best confessor will be unable to finally dissuade you from focusing on your reflection in the pond of pride. The surface of this pond, which was disturbed for a little while by the confessor's words, will become very smooth again and you will be able to peacefully return to your own occupation of admiring yourself.

What the narcissist has heard enriches his own vision of the world and his own image of God's will. For him, Christ's knocking will be effective only when it is heard according to what he wants to hear and, finally, Christ's knocking is forgotten.

THE ROOT OF NARCISSISM

The pond of the pride of human regard is the contaminated source into which a spiritual narcissist lovingly gazes at himself. The narcissist's main aspiration is to make a good impression or come across well, either from his own point of view or that of others. That is the context of the pond in which a narcissist constantly contemplates himself. In this pond he is looking for acceptance, recognition, or even admiration. Such is the goal that mobilizes the narcissist's strength or, contrarily, hides his weakness from other people. In this posture there is a constant **enslavement to the need to be accepted by others or one's self.**

You may ask yourself whether you have something of the narcissist within yourself. Is not how others – your family, your friends, your boss, or your acquaintances from work – evaluate and perceive you the most important to you? Or perhaps, do you count on yourself and judge how you come across to yourself? There is no big difference whether you consider yourself a conformist or you try to go against the trend of human opinions. In either case, if you are directed by your own beliefs, then your heart is closed to the Lord Who is knocking.

At the basis of your decisions is not the desire to be open to God's will, but rather, the **pride of human regard**. This pride rules over you. You become a marionette moved by the strings of its own pride. Such a puppet considers securing its own honor and good name as the most important thing in life. Such a person is ready to argue in his own defense with everyone and even give up his life to attain this goal. Sometimes such people torment their spouses with various demands because they want to make sure that everything goes according to their schedule, so that they appear successful before other people. They may even terrorize their children to act in ways that fulfill all of their expectations.

When you fall into the trap of the pride of human regard you behave according to your own personal whims and opinions or according to the wants and opinions of people who are important to you and who fulfill the role of idols in your life. You are not being led by what God expects from you at any given moment. Instead, you are directed to do something that you think you should do or say because of the criteria that **you have defined for yourself.**

THE WARPED DESIRE FOR FREEDOM

The spiritual narcissist desires to be free to the point that he is intoxicated by his great desire and does not even realize what enslavement entangles him. When you are closed before the "knocking" Light, Who desires to reveal to you the truth about the spiritual misery that fills the inner space of your soul's whitewashed tomb, with time, you become a slave to that within the shadows, which seems to you to be worthy of your love and servitude. You become a slave of your own phobias, habits, patterns of thinking, expectations, and demands of others.

Only when you follow the Love that unceasingly knocks on the human heart, can you experience the freedom that liberates you from a false image of yourself. When a person who is under the influence of a perverted desire for freedom turns his gaze from God and tramples on His will, he denies the truth that he is created in the image and likeness of God. Instead of striving after union with the Lord and becoming more like Him, the person chases after the illusion reflected in human eyes.

Professing the cult of worshiping one's own will and image, the spiritual narcissist inevitably strays away from God and wipes out the image of God in himself. You can realize your own likeness to God only to the extent that you fulfill not your own will, but God's will.

Surely you are free and nobody can force you to become like God. God fully respects your freedom. When you close yourself toward this "knocking" Love and you resist His grace, you cast yourself into a life of slavery to illusions connected to the false image of your own ego – your own *I*.

Freedom is something extraordinary and it takes on its proper meaning only in the posture that Mary assumed during the Annunciation. She was fully free, and yet with Her entire life She wanted to fulfill God's will – She wanted to become the handmaid of the Lord.

IN THE TRAP OF YOUR OWN EGOTISTICAL "I"

When you resist the Light of truth and you adore the false image of yourself, you become incapable of breaking yourself away from the cycle of your own egotistical *I*. A person who is in love with himself in a disordered way becomes a witness of his own tragedy because even his participation in the Eucharist or prayer can be manipulated in order to affirm his own visions.

A spiritual narcissist is incapable of fulfilling God's will without hindrance because he is constantly focused on fulfilling his own will. He becomes ensnared in his own trap that pulls him in like quicksand and from which it is very difficult to escape. A narcissist is not in a position to free himself from this trap because he subjects everything that could possibly help him to his own distorted perception. If the narcissist tries to free himself, then this only increases his enslavement to his own ego. As long as a narcissist remains floundering in this trap, he sentences himself to unnecessary suffering. All the while he feels lost because, although he does not feel a pang of conscience, he does not experience interior peace.

In spite of being in love with himself, the narcissist cannot fully accept himself. He is still not the kind of person he would like to be nor as he would like society to see him. He wants to be different than he is and, because of this desire, his contacts with other people leave him sad, lonely, and full of tension.

HOW TO FREE ONE'S SELF FROM NARCISSISM

In order to start to free one's self from narcissism, a person first has to admit to its existence. It is necessary to open one's self before the Divine light and, through it, to accept the unveiled truth about the interior of the whitewashed tomb full of the pride of narcissism.

You will not invoke this change in yourself unless you see that this light is love. God loves you to the point of folly and unceasingly knocks so that you can open the door to His love. Nothing discourages God. In order to forget about yourself, you first have to experience, at least to a small degree, God's crazy love. Only then will you be able to turn away from your own ego and direct your gaze in the direction of Divine light. When that happens, you will gradually begin to see the terrifying abyss that separates you – a narcissist – from God, Whose image is imprinted on the very bottom of your still resisting heart. You will discover the ugliness of the old person who consistently resists God as if he were chained in steel armor. However, when you discover God's love, a crack in this tightly sealed armor will appear – a crack through which a bright beam of light pierces the inside. The light will enable you to more fully discover Who God is and who you are. Only the folly of faith in God's love will allow you to dethrone the idol from your life – the idol that you strive to be for yourself and for others.

A person cannot live without love. It is love that gives meaning to our lives and our actions. Yet, the spiritual narcissist unceasingly looks for this love in precisely the wrong places, striving after human acceptance or self-acceptance. You will not turn away from your illusory self-image until you discover that Christ, Who is knocking on your door, loves you unlike anyone else because He knows the entire truth about your misery and your weaknesses. Instead, you will continue to resist God and try to escape from the truth about yourself.

TO CONSENT TO QUESTION YOURSELF

Only when you recognize how you are embraced by a great love, will your resistance to the light of God's truth melt away, and perhaps you will begin to turn away from the ugliness of the old self you have discovered in you. Perhaps one day you will come to a point described by St. Augustine, "love of God even to the contempt of self."[12]

Christ says, "Whoever loves father or mother more than me is not worthy of me, and whoever loves son or daughter more than me is not worthy of me" (Mt 10:37). God and His will are the most important. Perhaps, because of God, you will spurn your own narcissism, which demands that you constantly gaze at yourself, instead of opening the door of your heart to your Beloved Who desires to liberate you.

Perhaps, in response to God's tremendous love, which unceasingly knocks on the door of your heart, you will want to despise everything that enslaves you and imprisons you and you will want to turn away from your own ways of thinking and valuing yourself. Then, you will be ready to question everything from God's point of view: your concept of the world and life, your vision of your family, your work, and also the false image you have of yourself. Perhaps, you will also desire to live according to the true Gospel and you will reject the gospel according to Narcissus.

God's love demands your consent to question yourself and even to despise some part of your own ego. Jesus speaks very clearly when He says, "If your hand or foot causes you to sin, cut it off and throw it away. . . . And if your eye causes you to sin, tear it out and throw it away;" (Mt 18:8, 9).

---

[12] Augustine, *The City of God*, trans. Marcus Dods (New York: Random House, 2000), 14.28.

These words summon you to crucify the old person in you. Out of love for God, you should despise everything that is not of God. Pride, egoism, and enslavement to human regard distort, caricature, and deny God's image in you. These are the reasons why you frequently become a source of scandal for others. To some degree, your hard work can help you to change, but the ultimate transformation will happen only when you allow God Himself to transform you. As long as you turn away from the light of truth and are absorbed in admiring your own illusory image, you will be able neither to discover the old person in you nor recognize your false image of God. Therefore, you will not allow love to transform you.

WITH EMPTY HANDS

In order to help you to be liberated from admiring your own image, God can start knocking on the door of the kingdom of your inflated self image. In this way, He will deprive you of achievements that feed your pride. When you see that others are able to realize their plans and achieve success, whereas you are a constant failure, try to listen to God's knocking.

The Lord wants you to **stand before Him with empty hands**.[13] Perhaps it is best for you to see that you do very little, so that you can better come to know your weaknesses. Perhaps you will have to see that you cannot remain in truth, that you often lack good will, and that you always concentrate too much on yourself.

---

[13] St. Thérèse of Lisieux said: "At the evening of this life I shall appear before Thee with empty hands." Geneviève, *Memoir of My Sister*, 95.

Look to your Heavenly Father Who constantly bestows His grace on you; but, at the same time, understand that upon discovering this grace, He desires that you **live in the truth.** When you recognize some part of the supernatural good in your own life, try to remember that it belongs to God. With time, you will see more clearly the evil of which you alone are the author. Thanks to this outlook, you will see more easily that you are the only owner of your spiritual misery. You will also see that God is constantly present and active in your life. Then you will properly identify both good and evil. This will help you to remain in the posture of gratitude to God, while maintaining a necessary distance from yourself. Then it will be much easier for you to discover what God's will is for you and that you cannot realize even your own endeavors. You will be especially grateful to God for eliminating your own plans and for humiliating your pride. You will see this as the remedy that frees you from your enslavement to narcissism.

God has to disclose to you who you are, and He has to show you your insufficiencies. However, He cannot disclose everything about your spiritual misery to you if, upon seeing only a small part of the truth about yourself, you become sad and discouraged because what you discover does not match the vision of your own perfection or your false concept of the way to holiness. In this manner you limit the working of God. Only when you stand in truth before God and acknowledge everything that God discloses to you, will you be cured from your own interior conflict and will you receive inner peace.

WHEN YOU ABANDON THE POSTURE OF THE NARCISSIST

When you are no longer torn between the expectations of your Lord and those that you impose on yourself, you will begin to truly accept yourself. Only the person who is led by God's will is capable of accepting oneself:

> God, I am as You created me. If it is Your will that I embody this kind of character, appearance, way of being, then I say "yes" to it because You accept me and love me as I am. Certainly I do not want to be taken over by the opinions of others or even my own opinion of myself.

The person who concentrates on God and on fulfilling His will does not get too discouraged by his own failures, even when it comes to testifying to the truth. If others are not open to his words, his arguments, or his attitude, he tries to remember that faith is a grace, which these people perhaps have not yet received. Also, when he sees that he himself continually forgets about the truths pertaining to interior life, and when he does not see any of the fruits of his interior struggles, he tries to remember that God, in order to realize His will, can hide these fruits from him.

If God's will is truly the most important thing for you, and not human regard, then you will be preoccupied neither by the lack of results of your own efforts nor by what other people say about you. The only thing that will be important for you is that which God expects from you. In order to carry out God's will you have to abandon the pond of the pride of human regard. You will be unable to do this unless, like someone who is drowning, you reach out for the life vest of this truth: God loves you to the point of folly.

Remember that neither your sins nor your interior misery can change the fact that you are always God's beloved child. Even though you frequently do not accept yourself amid great doubts and darkness, you must not forget that God never rejects you. His Love unceasingly knocks even though you commit evil, even though you cannot do many things well, even though you cannot accept yourself, even though you so desperately look for success, and even though you constantly stand before the Lord with empty hands. This is what God wants. Perhaps, in this way, He is detaching you from human regard and waiting patiently for your "yes" — your consent to accept loneliness and misunderstanding by others — **so that finally you will discover His love.**

TO DISCOVER GOD'S IMAGE IN ONE'S SELF

Only when you cease to adore your own reflection in the pond of pride will you begin to be open to the Holy Spirit's action in you. In order to become more like God, you must turn away from your own ego and submit yourself fully to His will.

To submit to God means to live by the grace of Baptism, which gives us back our dignity as God's children and restores our likeness to our Father.

Christ's gifts of the Sacraments show us how much **God desires that we become more and more like Him**. Living by the graces of the sacraments: Baptism, Confirmation, Eucharist, Reconciliation, Matrimony or Priesthood, means to be open to God's humble knocking so that He may transform us and allow us to become more like Him. The extraordinary graces that we receive in the Sacraments can enable us to have this kind of supernatural relation to God, to another human being, and to one's self, especially with regards to the call that we have received from God according to our vocation.

Receiving these graces will enable you to adore God in the most profound way and realize your very likeness to Him. He desires to reflect His own image in the mirror of your soul.

TO FALL IN LOVE WITH THE LORD

When you stop appropriating God's gifts and His actions to yourself, you will more easily notice that Love is knocking on your door. This Love unceasingly takes care of you and becomes active in your life in more or less visible ways. Perhaps when this happens, you will daily discover anew the truth that Jesus safeguards you with the greatest care through all of your experiences. Then you will fall in love with God and you will cease to gaze at your own image.

When this happens, your concept of the need to always defend your own freedom will change. Your greatest treasure will become the imitation of the Blessed Virgin Mary, the humble servant of the Lord. You will be ready to defend your right to choose this concept of freedom, which means to become a servant and even a slave of the Lord. Departing from spiritual narcissism will allow you to spurn your former vision of God, the world, and yourself. You will be more open to a new vision of everything – the vision of a person who is in love with the Lord.

Surely, the old person in you will continue to resist God, affirming that you are simply enchanted by an unreal illusion. All of your faculties will entertain thoughts filled with skepticism: your mind, reason, memory, and experiences. However, your own will can reply that the real illusion is precisely a life without the folly of God's love. Lacking true faith to the point of folly signifies a compromise and, in the end, this compromise always leads to sin and consequently, to a deeper immersion into evil.

A BLESSED FAULT

If you do not try to be faithful to the end, according to the example of the humble handmaid of the Lord, then you will continue to just tread water in your interior life. You will not be able to take advantage of this inconceivable grace thanks to which even your faults and your sins cannot turn you away from God. At every moment you can start building anew that which, through your sinfulness, you destroyed. If you allow God's light to shine on it, each unfaithfulness can become an occasion for contrition and to deepen your humility, so that turning away from the adoration of your own image, each unfaithfulness can become a **happy fault**.

You should live your life thanking God for this most extraordinary grace – for the happy fault. God's response, after man's rebelliousness, is merciful, in accordance with St. Paul's words, "where sin increased, grace overflowed all the more" (Rom 5:20). If you do not believe in this, then you will remain in despair like Judas did. But, if you believe, then you will be able to confess your own evil to God in every moment and beg Him for forgiveness:

> I believe, God, that my faults can become happy faults. I want to begin everything over again. And from this new beginning, I want to be faithful to You like Mary. I want to be in love with You to the point of folly.

TO FALL IN LOVE WITH MARY

The easiest and surest way to arrive at falling in love with God is to fall in love with Mary first. When you fall in love with Her, you will want to disappear and to die to yourself like She did. You will desire that the false image of **your ego** in your heart be replaced by God's image. Likewise, you will then desire to be incapable of your own action, and instead you will desire to fulfill God's will, just as Mary did. In order for this to happen, you have to become aware of Her presence in you and Her actions through you in each moment of your life. You have to notice the goodness that She causes in your life.

Then you will live more in God's presence everyday. Perhaps then, you will admit that for all successes you achieve, from the biggest to the smallest, you are indebted to Mary.

And so will begin the process of detaching yourself from self-adoration and from gazing into the pond of the pride of human regard. You will be able to see your misery more easily; consequently, you will be liberated more and more from prideful and disordered self-love. For, liberation from one's self is the very essence of humility.[14]

You will experience the transforming grace of conversion in your life. Even though this miracle can be hidden from your sight for a long time, in the final account it is not so important that you see that you are changing. What is important is that this transformation proceeds according to God's will.

---

[14] Cf. von Hildebrand, *Transformation in Christ*, 150.

CHILDLIKE HUMILITY

"Behold, I stand at the door and knock. If anyone hears my voice and opens the door, [then] I will enter his house and dine with him, and he with me."

REVELATION, CHAPTER 3:20

Humility is the truth about yourself and the truth about God. The truth about you is that you receive everything from God. The truth about God is that He gives you everything and He wants to continue to bestow gifts upon you. He wants to do so, however, under the condition that you follow His command to be continually renewed in the posture of the **evangelical child** (see Mt 18:4) whose entire existence is a cry to God for His bestowals. Only childlike humility opens the door of a person's heart to God's knocking.

God, Who knocks on the door of your heart with the light of His truth, wants to show you that regardless of what you think about yourself – about your achievements or even about your social status – you are in reality only a small helpless child, who can do nothing on your own without Him. A person who is preoccupied with himself and turns his back on God's light is unaware of his own identity and lives in the illusion of his own might and self-sufficiency.

Only when various stages of the whitewashed tomb are consecutively exposed, will a person discover who he essentially is, especially in light of the outpouring of God's love over the world. But the truth about that which lies most deeply hidden within the murky recesses of our soul can terrify us.

The best medicine for the despair that inevitably appears under the influence of hopeless analysis of the ugly, filthy state of our whitewashed tomb is to maintain the posture of spiritual childlikeness. As you discover each new state of your whitewashed tomb, this posture will allow you to throw yourself into the arms of your Heavenly Mother. Spiritual childlikeness will enable you to thank Mary for loving you in spite of your misery. It is true that the interior of the whitewashed tomb is filthy and abominable. However, it is also true that you are loved not because of some kind of imaginary perfection or cleanliness of soul, but because you are a child – the Heavenly Father's child. He will always accept you. When you throw yourself into His arms with childlike trust, He will never despise you or abandon you.

TO STAND IN THE LIGHT OF TRUTH LIKE A CHILD

In evangelical symbolism, a little child is entirely preoccupied with calling out for help, for a bestowal, or for a rescue. The words of Jesus Christ, "unless you turn and become like children, you will not enter the kingdom of heaven" (Mt 18:3), take on a special significance in reference to those to whom God gives the grace of His own light of truth. This grace can be very difficult for us to receive because the truth that we discover, thanks to God's mercy, about our misery, is sometimes very shocking. It is easy to fall into despair when we see our inner self, the recesses of our whitewashed tomb, and how our life is leading us to ruin. God discloses the truth in order to heal a person. However, He does not want to impose Himself; therefore, He exposes our wounds and seems to ask us: *Do you want to be healed?*

You cannot be rescued if, upon seeing the hopelessness of your situation, you refuse to convert, and if, when excessively thinking about your wasted life and, more generally, about yourself, you refuse to call out for rescue like a child. If you need to ask, "How do I call out for rescue?" then you no longer have the posture of a little child; rather, you are playing the role of a child. A child simply calls out and screams as loudly as he can. A child knows that he cannot manage on his own; therefore, he calls on his father, whose arms are full of warmth, to point out the way of light. Then the father becomes like a boat of rescue in which the child can safely travel to the other side.

CHAPTER FIVE

THE CHILDLIKE POSTURE OF THE SAMARITAN WOMAN

As Jesus traveled through the land of Palestine, He singled out certain groups of people who were especially close to Him. Children pertained to this category. Jesus blessed them and held them up as examples of the need to be reborn. We have to return to the state of being childlike (cf. Mt 18:3), and we have to agree to be born again (cf. Jn 3:5). This process is difficult for us because of the pain that is associated with it.

We can assume that the Samaritan woman whom Jesus met by Jacob's well in Sychar was full of pain and suffering. The people of Samaria had rejected her because of her sins. Perhaps she was afflicted by the truth that her whitewashed tomb was filled with evil and filth. Nevertheless, she did not close herself up like a snail in its own shell. She did not give in to the temptation of bitterness. Perhaps, in the deepest recesses of her being, amidst all the pain of rejection, a small spark of hope smoldered – the hope that a rescue would come.

Jesus, in a posture full of patience and humility, talked to the Samaritan woman for such a long time that He pierced through the various levels of her being to that place where her hope and longing to be rescued flickered. And when, to her great surprise, she discovered someone who did not spurn her, did not reject her, and did not throw stones at her, she began opening herself to God's light that ever so delicately and humbly knocked on the door of her heart. Gradually, something new was born in her aching soul – something that turned her toward God's light – something of the posture of a child.

CHILDLIKE SIMPLICITY

Jesus' encounter with the Samaritan woman was something extraordinary. It was noon, when the scorching heat was at its peak; therefore, nobody would walk to the well to fetch water. And yet, who comes to the well seeking water? None other than an extraordinary Newcomer.

According to Jewish custom, a man was not allowed to speak to a foreign woman. Moreover, he was not supposed to ask such a woman for a drink of water or, for that matter, any kind of assistance:

> Jesus, tired from his journey, sat down at the well. It was about noon.
> A woman of Samaria came to draw water. Jesus said to her, "Give me a drink." His disciples had gone into the town to buy food.

The Samaritan woman said to him, "How can
you, a Jew, ask me, a Samaritan woman, for a
drink?" (Jn 4:6-9).

These first few words of the Gospel indicate that the
Samaritan woman was aware of her inferiority connected to
a certain trait of simplicity. It was this simplicity that
compelled her to openly ask this question that had formed
within her heart.

Upon seeing this woman's posture, Jesus struck up a
conversation, using words that made up a kind of riddle.
"Jesus answered and said to her, 'If you knew the gift of God
and who is saying to you, "Give me a drink," you would have
asked him and he would have given you living water'" (Jn
4:10). The Samaritan woman again asked a simple question,
which led to further clarification: "Sir, you do not even have
a bucket and the cistern is deep; where then can you get this
living water?" (Jn 4:11). At this moment, the posture of a
child was born in the Samaritan woman because when a
child does not grasp something, then a child asks a question
with pure simplicity. Then, when a child receives the answer
to his question, he accepts it because he believes what he is
told is true, even if he does not understand everything. The
Samaritan woman did likewise.

CHILDLIKE WISDOM

In response to the woman's question, "Jesus answered and
said to her, 'Everyone who drinks this water will be thirsty

again; but whoever drinks the water I shall give will never thirst; the water I shall give will become in him a spring of water welling up to eternal life'" (Jn 4:13-14). Once again, in Christ's words we can hear God's knocking – His dialogue was an invitation to the Samaritan woman. She responded with childlike wisdom by opening herself up to words that she did not fully understand even until the end of the dialogue. She received these words because they brought her wounded heart the hope of being rescued. And so, she responded, "Sir, give me this water, so that I may not be thirsty or have to keep coming here to draw water" (Jn 4:15).

This woman, rejected by society because of her sins, and filled with pain because of her own wretchedness, received Christ's answer with hope. She so desperately needed help and she so desperately needed to be rescued, that she was ready to believe that the words uttered by this extraordinary traveler, even though they seemed to be completely illogical, were indeed, completely true. How can a person who cannot live without water stop thirsting for it? Is this not against the law of nature? Only someone like the Samaritan woman, like a child hopefully awaiting a rescue, is able to receive the promise contained within Christ's words. It is precisely this childlike wisdom that prompted the Samaritan woman to take advantage of the situation; opening herself to God by asking Him for this extraordinary water.

Jesus noticed the Samaritan woman's increasing faith and accepted the invitation of this child who opened the door of her heart to Him. As a result, He revealed the extent of His omnipotent wisdom to her by conveying that He knew the truth about that which was hiding inside the whitewashed tomb of her soul. And so He commanded her, "Go call your husband and come back" (Jn 4:16). When the Samaritan woman responded that she did not have a husband, Jesus answered her, "You are right in saying, 'I do not have a husband.' For you have had five husbands, and the one you have now is not your husband. What you have said is true" (Jn 4:17-18).

Once again, we see the extraordinary simplicity in the posture of this sinful woman. The Samaritan woman did not try to hide the truth about her illicit relationship with the man with whom she lived. She answered Jesus *in accordance with truth*, saying that she did not have a husband, even though at that moment, she still did not know that Jesus knew all about her life. Responding in this way, the Samaritan woman did not close herself off to God's light which, although not yet shining in its fullness, was knocking, with increasing urgency, on the door of her heart. Then, very beautifully, in the next moment, she was finally convinced that this stranger, whom she was seeing for the first time, knew the truth about her crushing sin.

God's radiant light shone to such an extent that the Samaritan woman understood that a prophet stood before her. And how did she react to this light? Even in her unworthiness, she tried neither to justify herself nor run away ashamed. It was as if she turned away from herself, **looked beyond** the revealed truth about her sinfulness, and, with childlike wisdom, took advantage of the situation by posing a question to Jesus pertaining to her relationship with God, "Sir, I can see that you are a prophet. Our ancestors worshiped on this mountain; but you people say that the place to worship is in Jerusalem" (Jn 4:19-20).

Seeing this truth about the interior of her whitewashed tomb, the Samaritan woman was not preoccupied with her sins or herself; rather, she asked Jesus how she should pray and worship God. In response to such faith, Jesus revealed a very complex mystery to her. He announced to her a new reality, "Believe me, woman, the hour is coming when you will worship the Father neither on this mountain nor in Jerusalem. You people worship what you do not understand; we worship what we understand, because salvation is from the Jews. But the hour is coming, and is now here, when true worshipers will worship the Father in Spirit and truth" (Jn 4:21-23).

Jesus' answer was certainly unclear to the Samaritan woman. She received it, though, with childlike trust. She admitted her great faith a moment later by professing that when the Messiah came, He would manifest everything to human hearts. At that moment the light shone in its fullness and Jesus exclaimed to her: "I am he, the one who is speaking with you" (Jn 4:26). There must have been in the Samaritan woman a great hunger for God and for His grace because

Jesus was able to bestow such an extraordinary grace upon her. And, not only did he bestow this grace upon the Samaritan woman, but also upon those who had previously despised her.

THE LACK OF CHILDLIKE SIMPLICITY THAT CLOSES ONE TO REVELATION

Let us take a closer look at what further transpired at the well in Sychar. Let us consider what happened when the Apostles returned. Let us examine, if they, too, exhibited a posture of childlike trust: "At that moment his disciples returned, and were amazed that he was talking with a woman, but still no one said, 'What are you looking for?' or 'Why are you talking with her?'" (Jn 4:27). Unlike the Samaritan woman, the Apostles did not ask Christ the questions troubling their hearts. They were surprised by what they witnessed, but after the woman left, they did not ask Jesus their specific questions. Rather, ". . . the disciples urged him, 'Rabbi, eat.' But he said to them, 'I have food to eat of which you do not know.' So the disciples said to one another, 'Could someone have brought him something to eat?'" (Jn 4:31-33).

Does it not seem as if Jesus was trying to knock on the doors of His disciples' hearts in the same way that He had knocked, only a moment before, on the door of the heart of the sinful woman? Certainly, with childlike simplicity she would have taken advantage of this situation by immediately asking Jesus what kind of food she could eat with Him. The disciples, however, did not ask their Master any questions. They only *spoke among themselves*, most likely thinking according to **human logic** about how they should respond to Jesus. Every day they lived in the presence of God's light, but at this moment they lacked the childlike trust and simplicity that would have allowed them to be open to this light.

The Apostles' postures were similar to that of Nicodemus – the one to whom Jesus also tried to reveal this great mystery. But Jesus stopped talking with Nicodemus half-way through the conversation because He did not detect childlike simplicity in Nicodemus – the simplicity that calls out for God's bestowals. Jesus told Nicodemus, "Amen, amen, I say to you, no one can see the kingdom of God without being born from above" (Jn 3:3). And like the Apostles, Nicodemus received these words in a very rational way, responding "How can a person once grown old be born again? Surely he cannot reenter his mother's womb and be born again, can he?" (Jn 3:4). Nicodemus lacked the posture of faith and childlike simplicity and, because of this, Jesus was unable to reveal Himself to Nicodemus as He had revealed Himself to the Samaritan woman who, despite her living in mortal sin, completely opened her heart to Jesus. Perhaps her sinfulness interiorly crushed her so much that she was able to admit that she was like a helpless child and thus able to stretch out her hands with determination to the Lord.

Because of her sins, the Samaritan woman was rejected by the society in which she lived. When Jesus told her: "I am the Messiah," she did not consider the fact that she would face ridicule again. Therefore, she returned to her city without hesitation, proclaiming the One she met. Then something extraordinary happened: the inhabitants of Samaria not only refrained from ridiculing the Samaritan woman, they also came to Jesus and asked Him to remain with them. Two days later, the inhabitants declared before the Samaritan woman, "We no longer believe because of your word; for we have heard for ourselves, and we know that this is truly the savior of the world" (Jn 4:42).

And so, in contrast to the Samaritan woman, Nicodemus and the Apostles appeared to themselves to be without sin, and yet, they did not open their hearts to Jesus' words as the Samaritan woman did. When they approached Christ, their pride caused them to think not as God does, but as humans do. They were afraid to ask childlike questions. Nicodemus and the Apostles were not as clever nor as perfect as they wanted to appear to be. Instead of humbly opening their hearts to God's light, they tried to comprehend everything in a human way.

If someone is closed to God in this way, then he is unable to perceive supernatural reality. In addition, the supernatural reality cannot be revealed in its entirety to him. Only the evangelical child absorbs everything that God wants to bestow upon him. God is an unfathomable mystery. It is impossible to comprehend Him through human logic alone; rather, one must also have faith, trust, and childlike wisdom.

CHAPTER SIX

RECEIVING GOD'S KINGDOM LIKE A CHILD

A n attribute of love is the lowering of itself. St. Thérèse of the Child Jesus described this attitude in this way: "In order that Love be fully satisfied, it is necessary that It lower Itself, and that It lower Itself to nothingness and transform this nothingness into *fire*."[15] God's light, which is knocking in order for us to find out the truth about our nothingness, wants us to discover that this place to which we lower ourselves is the very place where God desires to meet us.

This Love, which knocks, becomes not only a light, but also a fire that desires to engulf us and to transform us into a flame. According to St. Thérèse, "Holiness does not consist in this or that practice; it consists in a disposition of the heart, which makes us always humble and little in the

---

[15] Thérèse of Lisieux, *Story of a Soul: The Autobiography of St. Thérèse of Lisieux*, 3rd ed. trans. John Clarke (Washington, DC: ICS Publications, 1996), 195. Translation of *Histoire d'une âme: manuscrits autobiographiques* (Editions du Cerf and Desclée de Brouer, 1972). Citation is from Manuscript B, 3v°, Letter to Sister Marie of the Sacred Heart. – Ed.

arms of God, well aware of our feebleness, but boldly confident in the father's goodness."[16]

God is knocking on your door because He wants you to acknowledge your own weakness and to boldly trust in His love. This Love that knocks will not refuse to bestow gifts upon the one, who, acknowledging his own helplessness, calls upon It.

A CHILD LOOKING AT THE WORLD THROUGH THE FATHER'S EYES

Jesus said that, in order to receive the kingdom of God, we have to receive it like a child. Parents were bringing their children to Jesus so He could bless them. The disciples did not want the children to annoy our Lord so they tried to prevent this. "When Jesus saw this he became indignant and said to them, 'Let the children come to me; do not prevent them, for the kingdom of God belongs to such as these. Amen, I say to you, whoever does not accept the kingdom of God like a child will not enter it'" (Mk 10:14-15).

If somebody wants to enter the kingdom of God, such a person must seriously consider the meaning of these words of Jesus Christ. If this person does not receive the kingdom like a child, such a person will not enter it, and will remain enclosed in the very tight borders of being ruled by his own *I*.

---

[16] Thérèse de Lisieux, *Novissima Verba: The Last Conversation and Confidences of Saint Thérèse of the Child Jesus, May-September, 1897,* rev. trans. Carmelite Nuns of New York (New York: P.J. Kenedy, 1952), 78.

We cannot be in both kingdoms at the same time. We must depart from one in order to receive the other – the one offered to us by God. Whoever does not receive the gift of God's kingdom will not enter it. Such a person is somewhere else, engaged in the kingdom of his own dreams and illusions. In order to receive the Lord, Who is revealing Himself to us, we have to let go of our dear illusions and stand before Him in truth, acknowledging that on our own we have nothing. Only when the posture of **childlike simplicity** appears in our interior life will we then be capable of depending totally, in everything, on God.

When they are small, children unreservedly trust their parents. From their parents, children learn about the world. A child looks at everything as if through the eyes of his parents. Children try to mimic their parents' opinions and accept their parents' ways of thinking and judging as their own. To receive God's kingdom like a child means to attempt to look at the world, other people, and finally one's self, in the same way as our Heavenly Father looks at us. What is His gaze like? Among other things, the challenge that Jesus directed to the Apostles during the Last Supper addresses this question: "I give you a new commandment: love one another. As I have loved you, so you also should love one another" (Jn 13:34). God's gaze is always loving. Jesus, relying on His love toward His disciples, calls them to imitate His love by loving others as He loves. It is not enough to love our neighbor as we love ourselves. We have to love as God loves. It is true that it is quite difficult for us to even love our neighbor as ourselves. This challenge of Christ to love others as God loves them can seem beyond our capability; but, for the evangelical child, nothing is impossible. Totally focused on the Father, the child looks at the world in the same way God the Father looks at the world. The evangelical child cherishes the Father's example and tries to imitate God in everything.

St. Thérèse of the Child Jesus in her childlike trust and simplicity admitted:

> Ah! Lord, I know you don't command the impossible. You know better than I do my weakness and imperfection; You know very well that never would I be able to love my Sisters as You love them, unless You, O my Jesus, *loved them in me.* It is because You wanted to give me this grace that You made your *new* commandment. Oh! how I love this new commandment since it gives me the assurance that Your Will is *to love in me* all those You command me to love! (Thérèse, *Story of a Soul*, 221. Citation is from Manuscript C, 12v° addressed to Mother Marie De Gonzague. – Ed.)

If you open yourself before God, then you allow Him to fill your inner self with His transforming light.

THERE IS ENOUGH GRACE FOR YOU IN ORDER TO LOVE

Jesus Christ knocks at your door by allowing you to encounter difficult and unpleasant people. He expects that you will try to fulfill His *new commandment*. You have to remember that He is not expecting the impossible from you. When somebody's behavior, actions, views, or posture is irritating to you, you have a special opportunity to be like a child who imitates his own Father in everything.

In the book, *The Imitation of Christ*, Thomas Kempis states that "It is better to avert your eyes from what distracts you from your purpose. Quietly leave each person to his own opinion and avoid contentious bickering."[17] It is easy not to quarrel in a discussion when we see that the person with whom we are speaking is right. It is very hard, though, to leave another person with his opinion when you are convinced that the person is wrong. It would be important then to be reminded how our Almighty God treats us when we are the ones who stray away and are in the wrong. Does He pressure us or stop loving us?

When, however, the demands of Christ seem very difficult, remember what God told St. Paul in a similar situation, "My grace is sufficient for you, for power is made perfect in weakness" (2 Cor 12:9). Jesus Christ calls us to love

---

[17] Thomas À Kempis, *The Imitation of Christ, Thomas À Kempis: A Timeless Classic for Contemporary Readers,* trans. William C. Creasy (Notre Dame, IN: Ave Maria Press, 1998), 135.

in a very real way, without any self-interest, the way He loves us. "Give to everyone who asks of you, and from the one who takes what is yours do not demand it back" (Lk 6:30). When we analyze this call of God, with proper simplicity, let us ponder the words of St. Thérèse of the Child Jesus:

> Giving to all those who *ask* is less sweet than offering oneself by the movement of one's own heart; again, when they ask for something politely, it doesn't cost so much to give, but if, unfortunately, they don't use very delicate words, the soul is immediately up in arms if she is not well founded in charity. She finds a thousand reasons to refuse what is asked of her, and it is only after having convinced the asker of her tactlessness that she will finally give what is asked, and then only *as a favor*; or else she will render a light service which could have been done in one-twentieth of the time that was spent in setting forth her imaginary rights. (Thérèse, *Story of a Soul*, 225. Citation is from Manuscript C, 15v°-16r°. – Ed.)

How often do we take something that belongs to God and He acts as if He does not notice? In reality, everything belongs to God. We, however, take something without ever asking God for it because we assume we have the right to it. God willingly gives when we ask Him for something. But He also gives when we take without asking.

If we, however, want to imitate our heavenly Father, we too should allow others to take what belongs to us, not only when they ask us for it, but also when they demand something in an unpleasant way. Normally, in such circumstances, we get upset and feel obliged to instruct such a person about their lack of good manners. We want to teach this person a lesson. We cannot allow somebody to show us such a lack of respect, can we? God treats us in a totally different way. The One who is pure Love does not expose us to many moral lessons. Instead, He frequently responds to us even when we demand instead of ask, even when we, who are creatures that alone are nothing, do not show the respect due to the Creator. The Merciful Creator of the Universe bestows gifts to everybody. He gives to those who negate His presence and, in so doing, reject Him. He continues to serve them, even though they despise Him. He fulfills various kinds of desires as if He were a slave. How extraordinary is the humility of God, for He does not pursue His own interests; rather, He always waits.

St. Thérèse of the Child Jesus writes that to give up one's own rights can become something very difficult when it comes to small things: "For example, in my work of painting there is nothing that belongs to me, I know. But if, when I am preparing for some work, I find that the brushes and the paints are in disorder, if a [ruler] or a penknife has disappeared, patience is very close to abandoning me and I must take my courage in both hands in order to reclaim the missing object without bitterness." [18]

---

[18] Thérèse, *Story of a Soul*, 226. Citation is from Manuscript C, 16vº. – Ed.

Scissors and rulers seem to be trivial things, but it is those trivial things, in various situations, where we find it most difficult to control certain reactions of our nature. When the mess that is left behind by your family members or co-workers upsets you, try to think about how God reacts when He sees the mess that we make in the world. He sees fully the horrible consequences of our straying from His will, but in His peculiar yet amazing love, He does not hurry to punish us. On the contrary, He patiently knocks on the doors of our hearts and continues to be very gentle toward us.

St. Thérèse writes:

There is no joy comparable to that which the truly poor in spirit experience. If such a one asks for something with detachment, and if this thing is not only refused but one tries to take away what one already has, the poor in spirit follow Jesus' counsel: *"If anyone take away your coat, let go your cloak also."*

To give up one's cloak is, it seems to me, renouncing one's ultimate rights; it is considering oneself as the servant and the slave of others. When one has left his cloak, it is much easier to walk, to run, and Jesus adds: *"And whoever forces you to go one mile, go two more with him."* Thus it is not enough to give *to everyone who asks*; I must even anticipate their desires, appear to be very much obliged and honored to render service, and if anyone takes

something which is for my use, I must not
appear to be sorry about this but happy at
being *relieved* of it. (Thérèse, *Story of a Soul*,
226-227. Citation is from Manuscript
C, 16vº-17rº. – Ed.)

To remain in this posture is very difficult. St. Thérèse, in her
childlike simplicity, believed that she would receive everything
from God, and she tried to imitate Christ in her own life. Her
attitude can be, for us, a very vivid image of the trust of a child
who realizes fully well that by herself she cannot love others,
but awaits everything from the Father Who is knocking on
her door with His strength, power, and love.

By giving us the new commandment to love one another
as He has loved us, Jesus Christ wants us to become **servants and,
as if, slaves of others**. A slave has the dignity of a child of God,
acknowledges he has no rights, and depends on the will of his
Master, the Lord, in everything. If the slave loses something
because of God's will, then he accepts this loss with joy, knowing
that it is an expression of the Lord's purest love that **frees him
from something that was unnecessary**. This posture was fully
realized by the Blessed Mother, who, by Her own example, allows
us to clearly understand the new commandment of love. When
Christ gives us this commandment, He is telling us to love the
other person as He loves this person, so that we die to ourselves
and embrace the Cross.

God bestows His love on everyone, even those who
persecute Him or crucify Him. If you want to imitate Him,

then you too should love the people who are a source of suffering and torment for you. St. Thérèse describes this for us:

> The Lord, in the Gospel, explains in what *His new commandment* consists. He says in St. Matthew: *"You have heard that it was said, 'You shall love your neighbor and hate your enemy.' But I say to you, love your enemies ... pray for those who persecute you."* No doubt, we don't have any enemies in Carmel, but there are feelings. One feels attracted to this Sister, whereas with regard to another, one would make a long detour in order to avoid meeting her. And so, without even knowing it, she becomes the subject of persecution. Well, Jesus is telling me that it is this Sister who must be loved, she must be prayed for even though her conduct would lead me to believe that she doesn't love me: *"If you love those who love you, what reward will you have? For, even sinners love those who love them."* St. Luke, VI. And it isn't enough to love; we must prove it. We are naturally happy to offer a gift to a friend; we love especially to give surprises; however, this is not charity, for sinners do this too. (Thérèse, *Story of a Soul*, 224-225. Citation is from Manuscript C, 15vº-16rº. – Ed.)

If you willingly help the people who are kind and good toward you, who understand and love you, then you are not doing anything extraordinary, even if you are capable of making great sacrifices. You then act as those who do not lean on God and do not take advantage of His special power.

The One Who is knocking expects something much more from you. If you invite Him to yourself in the posture of an evangelical child, and if you open up to Him the world of your difficult relationships with various persons, those whom you cannot love, He Himself will lead you with His light and **will teach you how to also love those who wound you.**

St. Thérèse writes about the extraordinary outcome of such love. She says, "It is only charity that can expand my heart."[19] If you open the door of your heart to the humble Christ, and try to imitate Him like a child, then your heart will *grow* and, without knowing it, you will become more like the One Who is Love.

IMITATING THE GAZE OF THE HANDMAID OF THE LORD

It is best if we learn from our Blessed Mother, Mary, how to look at the world and how to receive the kingdom of God like a child. She perceives everything the way God does and She loves every person in the same manner as God does.

Mary describes Herself as a handmaid, or servant, of the Lord. This statement has a very deep meaning. Today, a servant is not much worse off than the one who hires him. In the time of Christ, however, a significant social difference existed between a lord and his servant. Jesus told the Apostles, "I no longer call you slaves, because a slave does not know what his master is doing" (Jn 15:15). These words recall

---

[19] Thérèse, *Story of a Soul*, 226. Citation is from Manuscript C, 16r°. – Ed.

that during Christ's time the servant, like the slave, was uninformed about everything and was expected to accept this lack of knowledge. Mary resembled this type of servant precisely. The Mother of our Lord accepted Her lack of knowledge. She asked only for the things that were necessary in order to fulfill God's recommendations, in order to realize His will in fullness. This posture symbolizes that of the evangelical child who does not try to comprehend worldly matters because he knows that he cannot embrace everything. A child simply trusts in the Father and follows Him step by step, holding His hand, looking at the world through His eyes. Mary, at the moment of the Annunciation, became fully aware of Her own nothingness and so became completely reliant on God. In this way, She was like the evangelical child. Mary, the one who was full of grace (see Lk 1:28), stood before God in the posture of complete poverty. She had nothing and depended totally on God.

The call to childlike trust is always leading us to imitate Mary. Our Heavenly Father wants us to imitate the way Mary lowered Herself before Him, especially the way that She continually maintained the posture of servant and slave.[20] Mary assumes this posture because She knows that Her humility and childlike manner lead Her to abandon Herself to God's love – a love that is constantly knocking on the door of the human heart.

---

[20] "Behold, I am the handmaid of the Lord" (Lk 1:38). The Greek text speaks about the "slave of the Lord," thus implying a person who is a possession of his owner. As a "thing," in the hands of his owner, a slave has no rights and no freedom. Therefore, the will of God is also the will of a slave or handmaid of the Lord. In other words, the handmaid or slave always wants to fulfill God's will.

TO GAZE UPON CHRIST LIKE A CHILD

Christ stands at your door and knocks unceasingly so that you will constantly see that you always were, always are, and always will be, a child who is weak, helpless, and unable to manage without God. Upon realizing your own powerlessness, you may then acknowledge that, on your own, you will never be able to look at the world as God does, or to love as God does. You should remember, however, that it is precisely your nothingness that is unconditionally loved, even to the point that Jesus gave up His life on the Cross for you.

The light of God's grace that reveals the inside of your whitewashed tomb, does not want your soul to be paralyzed by the dirtiness of this shocking scene. Rather, the goal is to allow yourself to be healed so that you may turn your gaze away from yourself and gaze with gratitude upon Christ. It is important to cling to Him and not to focus too much on what you see within the whitewashed tomb.

Only God, the One Who redeemed your misery and transformed it, is important. He redeemed all the filth that you discovered, acknowledged, and recognized as your own before Him. You should not be preoccupied with it any longer. Like a child, begin to await everything from Him because, as St. Thérèse tells us, "As we hope in Him so shall we receive."[21]

When you recognize the abyss of your own misery and discover the abyss of God's love, then you may try to become like a servant and slave of the Lord. Then it will be much

---

[21] Thérèse de Lisieux, *Saint Thérèse of Lisieux: The Little Flower of Jesus*, rev. trans. Thomas N. Taylor (London: Burns Oates & Washbourne LTD, 1944), 232. Translation of *Counsels and Reminiscences*.

easier for you to agree that, just as a slave, **you do not have to understand everything**, and you do not have to know why God deals with you in this or that way. The more you know and understand, the more you are in danger of becoming possessive of God's gifts and your pride may increase.

The servant who receives everything and accepts everything becomes like a child who is absorbed in looking at the father and imitating all of his moves. The evangelical child imitates the Heavenly Father in everything, including His look, gestures and attitude. You need this attitude very much. When you gaze upon Christ like a child, you will begin to love like He loves, the way He loves you from the Cross.

TO LOOK AT THE WHITEWASHED TOMB WITH THE EYES OF AN EVANGELICAL CHILD

The mystery of the whitewashed tomb is best received in the posture of an evangelical child. How does this child react upon seeing something so shocking? Screaming, the child runs into the arms of mommy or daddy. Such a child knows only one particular answer for all of his problems. Whether he falls in a pothole full of mud, destroys a toy, tears his clothing, or gets into trouble, he always runs to mommy or daddy. The child does not think or become preoccupied with his appearance. The child does not worry about what will happen as a result. He does not calculate whether he is worthy of love or not.

The evangelical child will not shut the door on the knocking Father. He does not doubt his Father's love, even though the Father's knocking may mean very difficult and painful situations or experiences. It is true that there are children who are distrustful and sad, whom we can call "old." Such children, after each fall, focus on themselves and begin to consider: "Can I stand before mommy in such a state? Perhaps I should first clean myself up. Well, what will daddy think about me?"

Evangelical children react differently. When they are dirty, they do not take into account that they are unworthy to be embraced by their mommy. They still run into her open arms and do not attempt to be rescued by their own efforts. Even if you are under the impression that you have fallen into the sewer, and are totally covered from head to toe, do not waste any time contemplating this situation. The experience of your own misery is given to you precisely so that, without hesitation, you will throw yourself into the arms of your Blessed Mother. You should not doubt that She would receive you with great joy. Only then, when you are embraced and quieted as **a child in the arms of God, can you and should you think about your misery**. Do not do it, however, until you find yourself in those arms because, on your own, you will stop half way, and you will not take advantage of the fullness of God's Mercy. Only a child, trustfully clinging to Daddy, can take complete advantage of His mercy. "Amen, I say to you, unless you turn and become like children, you will not enter the kingdom of heaven"

(Mt 18:3). Children run fastest toward holiness. If you become like a child, it will be much easier for you to rise above the pride that is manifested in a special way through your discovery of the truth about your whitewashed tomb.

DO NOT BECOME DISCOURAGED BY YOUR MISTAKES

In order to remain like a child before God, we cannot get discouraged by the truth that God's light reveals to us about our numerous mistakes and negligences. St. Thérèse of the Child Jesus says, "To be small is not . . . to become discouraged over one's faults, for children fall often, but they are too small to hurt themselves very much."[22]

For many of us, this advice of St. Thérèse is very difficult. Often our smallest failure, stumble, or fall, leads us to discouragement, doubt, and sadness. The reason for this lies in the fact that we are concentrating too much on our own unfaithfulness and imperfection and not enough on God's goodness and love.

Every fall becomes a fiasco for the person who does not believe in love. If you believe that God is always with you, and **looks upon you with great love even when you fall**, you will try to get up right away. You will be like a small child who is learning how to walk: the child falls to the ground and immediately picks himself up. Because he is small like an evangelical child, this fall will not cause him too much pain.

---

[22] Thérèse, *Her Last Conversations*, 139.

The greater, more prideful, and more self-assured we are, the more difficult our falls will be. However, God's child who, after each fall, is aware of his helplessness reaches out his hands toward the Father. The sense of weakness and trust prompts the child to unceasingly call upon God. The child knows that he is feeble and clumsy, but the child also knows the One Whom he can constantly lean and call upon for his rescue. The child does not concentrate too much on his unfaithfulness, but all of his attention remains focused on the One Who loves him. The child falls many times, but each time he gets up to start life with new hope.

Until you stop believing in your own strength and stop wanting to rely on your own merits, you will not be able to take advantage of God's light that shows you who you really are. The evangelical child leans on grace and God's love and believes that God, if He so desires, will crown all of his efforts with victory. St. Thérèse says, "I am far from being on the way of fear; I always find a way to be happy and to profit from my miseries."[23] Because of the constant knocking of Love, St. Thérèse wanted to respond most of all with the posture of boundless trust. This posture can be expressed in the words, *I will get up from my misery and I will go to the Father.*

St. Thérèse wanted to base her dialogue with God on her misery, helplessness, and nothingness. Whenever she perceived that she was preoccupied with herself and lost in

---

[23] Thérèse, *Story of a Soul,* 173. Citation is from Manuscript A, 80r°. – Ed.

the "trifles of earth," she immediately turned back toward her "beloved Sun" in order to recount in detail all her infidelities.[24] She was convinced though, that by her bold trust, she would win over the greater Love, the One Who *came to call sinners to repentance and not the self righteous* (cf. Mk 2:17). She was like a child who "truly loves his parents and, since he is powerless and weak, he has no other thought than to abandon himself to them entirely."[25] Those were her special encounters with the Father. In order to explain this unshakeable trust that St. Thérèse had in God, her sister Céline recalls in her memoirs that her sister Thérèse used to say, "Can a father scold his child when the child is the first to own up to his fault? . . . Certainly not. He just presses the little one to his heart."[26] In her bold trust, St. Thérèse was convinced that **upon acknowledging the guilt of her faults before God Who loves her, she would be loved even more after the fall than before the fall.**

To one of her novices, who came to her and asked for her forgiveness for something that the novice had done wrong, St. Thérèse said:

> "If you knew how I feel! . . . Never have I more clearly understood the love with which Jesus receives us when we seek His forgiveness. If I, His poor little creature, feel so tenderly towards you when you come back to me, what must

---

[24] Thérèse, *Story of a Soul*, 198-199. Cf. Manuscript B, 5rº. – Ed.
[25] Geneviève, *Memoir of My Sister*, 59.
[26] Ibid., 59.

pass through Our Lord's Divine Heart when we return to Him? Far more quickly than I have just done will He blot out our sins from His memory. Nay, He will love us even more tenderly than before we fell." (Thérèse, *Saint Thérèse: Little Flower*, 310.)

TO HUMBLE ONESELF LIKE A CHILD IN ORDER TO MAKE ROOM FOR THE LORD

The road to our second nativity – becoming a child of the Gospel – is not easy. It is a lengthy process during which God teaches us to think and to act in new ways, while He gradually replaces the deeply rooted tendencies of the old person within us.

At the beginning of this road, God appears as light that illuminates the darkness of our soul and draws the soul with the brightness of the only truth. The old person does not give up and is constantly renewed in us. In order to defeat the old person, God intervenes in the life of the soul with a stronger light, which can finally become so forceful that it begins to blind, crush, and disable the human mind that resists it. The reason, unenlightened by faith, proves to be a continuous obstacle because until it is purified of its various attachments, it is unprepared for the radical transformations that are connected to sharing in the eternal life of God. When the mind is blinded by Divine Light, the soul begins to experience temptations against faith, crises, and trials of faith. St. John of the Cross refers to these experiences as the dark night of faith.

God's purifying action restores the proper dimensions to man. The mind's helplessness, when faced with God's paralyzing light, allows us to discover on the one hand, how great and inconceivable God is and, on the other hand, to recognize the smallness and helplessness of man. Then the soul is really born into the state of childlikeness. The person who is incapable of understanding God has a chance to open up more deeply to God's will, which is often incomprehensible. This entails a growing polarization: either the risk of retreating – *I do not understand you, God* – or greater openness to the will of God Who violently pounds on the door of a soul so that it will open up to Him.

The Gospel shows us an extraordinary example of someone who did not collapse in the face of trials of faith, but rather demonstrated an ever-increasing faithfulness to God's will. This is the example of St. John the Baptist, whom Jesus described with highest praise. If evangelical childlikeness is the desire to diminish one's self in order to make room for God, then we can say that John became smaller and smaller until he disappeared completely. Faithful to God's light, John the Baptist lowered himself completely in order to make room for the coming Lord. To lower one's self means to finally become a child – to reach the bottom of one's own nothingness so that God may become Everything.

With your mind fixed on the extraordinary posture of John the Baptist, you should also try to humble yourself in this deep way so that, like the evangelical child, you will make room for God. Try to humble yourself so that God can reign in your soul just as He reigned in the childlike soul of John.

Christ knocks on the door of your heart not only to enlighten you, but also to call you to humility, to make more room for God, because God can only reign fully in a truly humble soul.

CHAPTER SEVEN

"HE MUST INCREASE; I MUST DECREASE"

By lowering himself, John the Baptist was not limited only to making room for the coming Messiah and giving up his public activities. Thanks to Jesus' surprising attitude toward John – surprising from a human point of view – this great prophet progressed in lowering himself. When John the Baptist found himself in prison, he was humbled not only by his lack of personal freedom but also by his lack of understanding regarding what was happening to him and around him.

SO THAT GOD CAN ACT THROUGH US

When John the Baptist was told that, "the one . . . , to whom you testified, . . . is baptizing and everyone is coming to him" (Jn 3:26), he answered and said, ". . . He must increase; I must decrease" (Jn 3:30).

The words of John the Baptist indicate the way by which we can lead others to open the door to Christ. We have to lower ourselves and disappear, to become small like children of the Gospel, in order to make room for the Lord.

It is unusual that, regarding the necessity to *lower one's self*, Christ emphasizes the one whom He Himself called great: ". . . among those born of women, no one is greater than John" (Lk 7:28). The entire greatness of this prophet was, however, that he removed himself; he was willing to cast himself into the shadows and be forgotten.

John, who dedicated his life to announcing the coming of the Messiah and to preparing the chosen nation for His coming, spoke only once with Jesus – when Jesus asked John to baptize Him. Then, as recorded by John the Evangelist, the next day Jesus Christ passed John by, as if incidentally, and took his disciples from him. Upon hearing John's testimony of Jesus: "Behold, the Lamb of God, who takes away the sin of the world. . . . Now I have seen and testified that he is the Son of God" (Jn 1:29, 34), John's disciples began to abandon him.

Jesus did not visibly demonstrate any gratitude or special interest in John. He did not call John to follow Him. On the contrary, He left His most faithful herald in loneliness and uncertainty.

As the Gospel recounts, when John the Baptist was in prison, Jesus withdrew to Galilee. During this period, John the Baptist's uncertainty deepened even more because he did not understand the meaning of Jesus' deeds, about which others relayed to him in jail. John even sent his disciples to Jesus with a dramatic question, "Are you the one who is to come, or should we look for another?" (Mt 11:2).

From where did John's doubts come? After all, was he not the person who heard God's voice from heaven during Jesus' baptism saying, "This is my beloved Son, with whom I am well pleased" (Mt 3:17)?

These doubts can be understood when we consider how profoundly John's conception of the Messiah was rooted in certain Jewish expectations. After all, John had been calling out, "Even now the ax lies at the root of the trees. Therefore every tree that does not bear good fruit will be cut down and thrown into the fire. . . . The one who is coming after me . . . will baptize you with the holy Spirit and fire" (Mt 3:10-11). This great, ascetic prophet expected Jesus to begin His mission with a baptism of fire, which means, with a very severe judgment and punishment of sinners, or those who were against making the path of the Lord straight. That which was reported to John about Jesus' deeds did not conform to this image. John also needed to become like a child and therefore, the messianic mystery was partially hidden from him.

How great John's loneliness must have been in prison. Despite this loneliness, however, the entire time he lived in the spirit of his own words: "He must increase; I must decrease." John the Baptist wanted to decrease on behalf of Christ, **even though he understood Him less and less.**

Forgotten by those who had listened to him in the past, he accepted being forgotten by Jesus and he accepted that he did not fully understand Him. Deprived of Jesus' interest in him – the very same Jesus to whom John himself had witnessed – John must have felt abandoned and forgotten not only by others, but also by the Son of God.

John's loneliness resembles Christ's loneliness at the Garden of Olives and His spiritual darkness on the Cross, from which He called out to the Father: "My God, my God, why have you forsaken me?" (Mt 27:46). When John died a martyr's death, Christ's Sacrifice had not yet happened. However, because he was abandoned and because he experienced spiritual darkness, John was able to unite himself with the Crucified Christ in the most perfect way. John prepared the Chosen People to receive Christ's messianic message not only by his teachings, but also by the example of his life.

John the Baptist also wants to teach you something very important: in order for Christ to grow in you and in others, you must first die to yourself.

SO THAT I MAY NOT CONCEAL CHRIST

Apostolic work does not prevent us from contemplating ourselves in the pool of the pride of human regard. It does not shield us from striving to attain the recognition of others.

Do you not catch yourself sometimes wanting to impress others or win their esteem? Or, are you indifferent to the fact that your words and behavior evoke others' sympathy, respect or gratitude?

In each one of us there is a very strong desire to gain the approval of others, to be noticed by them, and to be held in their high esteem. The human *I* demands that it be in first place. It continuously wants to reflect its own ideal image in the eyes of others and it does not want to be small like a child. If you do not oppose these aspirations, then you are taking the place that belongs to Christ; **you conceal Him within yourself.**

Meanwhile, John the Baptist teaches that the greatest joy for an apostle is to see that Christ increases while he or she decreases on behalf of Him.

It is not easy to decrease and disappear in such a way that nobody will remember or miss you. St. John the Baptist spoke about rejoicing greatly when his disciples and the multitude of his flock abandoned him to follow Jesus. However, the opposite aspirations are within each person.

Our apostolate, nevertheless, becomes authentic and fruitful only to the degree to which we do not allow our *I* to occupy the place belonging only to Christ.

If you want your human heart to open up before the One Who is knocking, then you cannot occupy His place. You must decrease. You must convert and become like a child (cf. Mt 18:3). Only then will Christ increase in you and in the persons to whom you want to give Him.

If you try to become a mere **instrument** in His hands and **less and less visible**, then Jesus Himself will begin to carry out His work through you in the world.

The instrument must disappear in order for God to shine.

DISAPPEARING AS A GIFT AND A HELP TO OTHERS

On your road to holiness, the moment may arrive when, thanks to the light of grace, you discover that you should step aside and disappear from someone's life so that he may more easily find his support in Christ. If the attachment is strong between you, then this decision can be very difficult and misunderstood from a human point of view.

Why should you leave a person for whom you are a support or someone who is a support for you? How is the person going to understand this? Will it not seem to him something inhumane?

In this suffering and being torn you can seek light in the words of John the Baptist, "He must increase; I must decrease." John knew he had to back off and give his disciples over to Jesus. Did he fully understand, though, why he himself could not follow Christ like the Apostles? Did he understand why he had to step aside precisely in this way, without any explanation? In fact, nobody explained this to him nor did he have a chance to talk to Jesus. Surely he was torn as well. After all, he had lived in order to meet the Messiah and to serve Him. But when Christ came, John had to leave. This was exactly what God expected from John. If he had refused to step aside, then he would have become an obstacle to the action of grace, as well as to the process of increasing the One whose coming he had foretold. God can also expect something similar from you.

For both individuals, stepping aside and disappearing from the life of someone dear to us can be as painful as dying. In our hearts, something actually does die, and yet all the while we each want to live because human nature rebels against death.

However, can you permit yourself to conceal Christ? Can you agree to become an obstacle for His growth in the soul of another person? A person whose heart is attached to you cannot be open to God Who is knocking on his door. In order for Christ to increase, you may have to disappear, even if your friend is convinced that you do not hinder him and thinks, on the contrary, that you actually help him to be open to Christ.

When your feelings rebel (which is quite understandable), remember that the decision of your will is the most important to God. He wants you to make **seeking His will** the foundation of all your important decisions. Otherwise, your conscience will soon reproach you for your unfaithfulness and, after one arbitrary decision, a whole avalanche of others may occur. This is the biggest danger because such an avalanche can sweep you away and hurl you to rock bottom. In order to avoid succumbing to the temptation of willfulness, which has dangerous consequences, it would be good for you to make this kind of decision in strict cooperation with your confessor.

If you do everything to avoid concealing Christ from another person, then this person's relationship with the Lord will be able to deepen, even at the expense of his loneliness and certain woundedness. God will then impart to you the joy to which St. John the Baptist testified: ". . . the best man, who stands and listens for him, rejoices greatly at the bridegroom's voice. So this joy of mine has been made complete" (Jn 3:29).

The consciousness that Christ can increase in the heart of someone who is opening up to Him thanks to your decreasing, will become your **greatest joy.**

MEETING WITH THE LORD IN TRUTH

Within us, the greed of being *somebody* is very strong. This seemingly limitless desire confers upon us a certain importance and authority. You may even be ready to open the door to God, Who is knocking, and to welcome Him into your own life, but only under the condition that you do not lose too many of your feelings of self-worth. Willingly you will agree that God is *Somebody* very great – much greater than you

– while, you are also *somebody*, perhaps very small, but still *somebody* who has the right to be treated appropriately.

This greedy desire to be *somebody* is contrary to gratuitous love, to being loved **for nothing** in return. We want to be loved, but loved in return for something – in return for what we can give to God and to others. But can we be loved for nothing in return? This, indeed, seems very difficult to accept.

Deluding ourselves by thinking that we have to pay back for God's love, we steal God's glory from Him by attributing to ourselves that which is not ours. This greed that resides somewhere in the depth of our hearts and steals God's glory, does not want to be indebted to God for everything.

Our Heavenly Father cannot accept that by attributing His gifts to ourselves, we use them as adornments for our own crowns. When we do so, God has to back off. Even if we open the doors to Him, He will not enter because this openness is false.

In our relationship with God, praise belongs only to one of two sides, and we are not that side. Praise belongs to God alone. In order to be free to participate in His glory, we must admit that the kingly robes and shiny diadems that we wear are merely fake.

It is necessary for us to stand before the Lord in truth, as we really are – as weak and powerless children who constantly need His help. We must stand in truth as children who are not only weak, but often evil and greedy for greatness – greedy to steal God's glory from Him. We are the children who constantly need His forgiveness in order to become who we really are. This means that we need His forgiveness in order to stand in truth. Thanks to this standing in the truth, we can discover the great care with which we are being surrounded and the great love that is being outpoured on us on behalf of the One for whom we are a true treasure.

THE LORD COMES OUT TO MEET YOU

"Gird your loins and light your lamps and be like servants who await their master's return from a wedding, ready to open immediately when he comes and knocks" (Lk 12:35-36). How can we interpret this call to vigilance and readiness for the Lord's coming? Is it only an appeal to be ready for our meeting with the Lord at the moment of death?

The Lord wants you to await meeting with Him all the time – in every moment. After all, He is always standing at your door and knocking. He wants to meet with you during the day and during the night, in joy and in sorrow, in extraordinary events and in the monotonous rhythm of daily life.

He is present in you, around you, and
through everything that He created.

He is knocking on your door through
great and small events.

He is present in His will, which He
desires to reveal to you.

Are you the vigilant servant who hears the Lord's knocking? Do you run to the door to open it for Him?

The servant who is vigilant not only has *girded loins* in order to be ready to fulfill the Lord's indications, but also a *lighted torch*, which is the Light of Truth. Openness to God means, above all, **remaining in truth**.

MEETING IN TRUTH

To remain in truth means to attribute every supernatural good in your life to God. It means to give up all delusions that this goodness is yours.

To remain in truth means to attribute to yourself only spiritual misery[27] and the fact that you are frequently closed to God Who constantly comes forth to meet you. These elements condition your openness to God, but they are not enough. Upon seeing your spiritual misery, you should not

---

[27] The meaning of the expression "spiritual misery" is introduced in the words of R. Garrigou-Lagrange: "Finally, while humility, which recognizes our indigence, should be found in all the just and should be in the innocent man, it is after we commit sin that we recognize practically not only our indigence, but our wretchedness: the baseness of our selfish, narrow hearts, of our inconstant wills, of our vacillating, whimsical, ungovernable characters; the wretched weakness of our minds, guilty of unpardonable forgetfulness and contradictions that they could and should avoid; the wretchedness of pride, of concupiscence, which leads to indifference to the glory of God and the salvation of souls. This wretchedness is beneath nothingness itself since it is a disorder, and it occasionally plunges our souls into a contemptible state of abjection." Réginald Garrigou-Lagrange, *The Three Ages of the Interior Life: Prelude of Eternal Life*, vol. 2, trans. M. Timothea Doyle (St. Louis, MO: B. Herder Book Co., 1948), 121.

run away and hide from God as our first parents did; rather, you should constantly make an effort of the will to **be in the presence of God.**

What matters is that you open the door of your life and your heart to God and invite Him to enter into everything that you still consider yours so that it can all become more and more His kingdom.

Your mere effort is important, not the effects of that effort.

With the entire engagement of your will, try to stand in God's presence and simultaneously accept that all of your attempts will fail if the Lord does not preserve you from this. "Be like a child ... determined to climb a flight of stairs. Time after time it tries to set its tiny foot upon the lowest step, and each time it stumbles and falls."[28]

TO CONSENT TO FAILURE

Your consent to the failure of your efforts on the path to sanctity is essential. When God performs some miracles in your life out of love for you, try not to usurp them. Instead, try to acknowledge that on your own, you have only chaff and waste, whereas, the grain of supernatural good belongs only to God. Do not be afraid to acknowledge this – He will not reject you.

When you renounce your false greatness, you will become like the evangelical child. After all, by your own

---

[28] Thérèse, *Saint Thérèse, Little Flower*, 293.

strength you are incapable of being faithful to God, of being constantly open to His knocking. So, acknowledge your powerlessness and with childlike trust stretch out your hands to the Lord, asking Him for mercy. You can call out:

> *Lord, I do not make my own efforts in order to be successful because I know that by myself I am incapable of achieving them. I only want to come out to meet Your will and, because of that, I agree to accept every failure if You, in Your mercy, will not shield me from it.*

Try to stand in truth before God and try to come out to meet Him, in spite of the consciousness that you do not have sufficient faith or trust.

When your efforts are crowned with success, try not to attribute it to yourself. It does not make sense to feed your illusion that you are capable of generating supernatural good, like remembering God or living in His presence in your daily life, by yourself. That is why you should pray very clearly:

> *Lord, it is not I but You. You always come out to meet me first. You seek me. You knock on my door. You are faithful, not I.*

Naturally, to some degree each one of us is a co-creator of the good that God accomplishes in our lives. Nothing will happen to you, however, if you overlook your own contribution.

When you stand in truth before God and stretch out your hands toward Him with trust, you open yourself to the gift of Redemption. A sinner who asks for this gift always receives it. When you make room in your heart for the Lord by standing in truth, you allow Him to enter. You allow the One to enter Who, with the power of His Redemptive Sacrifice, can transform you and perform the incredible miracle wherein your useless chaff will be changed into life-giving grain.

THE MIRACLE OF WALKING ON THE WATER

The story in St. Matthew's Gospel about how St. Peter walked on the water demonstrates the consequences of attributing God's action to oneself. This happened during the fourth watch of the night, which means at dawn. When the Apostles were navigating toward the other side of the lake, they saw someone walking on the water. They were scared because they thought it was a ghost. Nevertheless, Peter said, "Lord, if it is you, command me to come to you on the water" (Mt 14:28). And He answered, "Come" (Mt 14:29).

The Evangelist noted that the wind was blowing against the boat and that the boat, being tossed by the waves, was quite far from the shore. St. Peter's decision to start walking toward Jesus demanded **folly of faith**. When St. Peter was coming out of the boat, he must have had the posture of the **evangelical child** because only such a child can believe in something that strongly denies all reason and experience – such as walking on water.

It seems obvious that a person cannot walk on water. Peter, however, believed that it was possible because Jesus called out to him, "Come."

When his feet were placed steadily on the waves, the Apostle must have understood that a real miracle was taking place. Perhaps he also realized that Jesus was performing this miracle despite his weak faith or even his incredulity and lack of trust. The experience of being touched by God, expressed by this miracle, must have provoked in Peter the deep sense of his own sinfulness. Perhaps he felt as he did when he caught the miraculous amount of fish – the event which coincided with Jesus calling him to become an apostle. On that occasion, Peter, being surprised by what Jesus did, fell down to his knees and said, "Depart from me, Lord, for I am a sinful man" (Lk 5:8).

We may assume that when Peter was walking on water he deeply experienced his own nothingness as well as the greatness of God, Who was touching him. Precisely because of this, he could not remain passive. Each time Peter took a step closer to Christ, he had to renew his effort to proceed.

With each step, perhaps Peter struggled with himself in order to remain in truth and not usurp this miracle or attribute to himself this faith which moves mountains and trust that suspends the laws of nature.

After each step, perhaps he humbly acknowledged before Jesus:

Lord, You make it possible for me to come to You by walking on water. I know that my faith and trust are very weak and You, in spite of everything, allow me to experience this miracle. I want to undertake this effort and to walk toward You anew. I accept though, that in every moment I can start drowning if You do not continue to suspend the laws of nature for me.

And the miracle continued.

THE SIGN OF DROWNING

At a certain moment, why did Peter give into his fear of the wind and begin to drown? Perhaps he lacked childlike humility and trust. Perhaps he ceased to remain in truth before God and appropriated the miracle to himself instead. Perhaps he began to place too much emphasis on his own cooperation with grace and, in this way, diminished the Lord's action. Or, perhaps when he started to feel that he was "somebody who knows how to walk on water" – a very important and mighty person – he ceased to be an evangelical child. Maybe there was no longer room in Peter's heart for Jesus, Who was performing this miracle.

After all, he would not have started to drown if he had tried to remember the entire time that he was walking on water despite his little faith and lack of trust. If he had remembered to keep in mind Christ's Love, then he could have tried to walk further by **relying only on Jesus** and not on himself.

At a certain moment, perhaps Peter started to wonder: "Will I be able to handle this? The wind is strong! The water is so rough! I am too far from the boat. How will I be able to continue walking farther?" **I**.

When the accent is placed on our *I*, we stop remaining, with the effort of the will, in the presence of the Divine *You*; we stop walking toward Christ and relying on Him. As a result, we start drowning because we are overwhelmed by the "waves" of life's adversities as well as our own spiritual misery.

When the terrified Peter began to be engulfed by the waves, "he cried out, 'Lord, save me!' Immediately Jesus stretched out his hand and caught him, and said to him, 'O you of little faith, why did you doubt?'" (Mt 14: 30-31).

REMAINING IN TRUTH, GO OUT AND MEET THE LORD

What happened to St. Peter shows us how much depends on our effort to remain in truth.

Remaining in truth prepares us for our meeting with Christ.

Christ wants to perform miracles in our lives, small or big, without fearing that we will trample upon these miracles and appropriate them to ourselves. For, if we do this, then we must suffer the humiliating experience of drowning. The story of St. Peter shows us that appropriating God's action to ourselves leads to humiliation. In fact, the near-drowning of Peter happened in front of the eyes of the other Apostles, who certainly heard Jesus' admonishment: "O you of little faith, why did you doubt?"

As long as you do not want to humble yourself before God and make room in your heart for His omnipotence, you make it impossible for Him to work extraordinary signs and miracles through you; you are too "old" and too self-assured.

Only by remaining in truth will you become a servant who is always ready to open the door to the Lord Who is knocking and allow Him to enter with His power into every situation of your life.

"If anyone hears my voice and opens the door, [then] I will enter his house and dine with him, and he with me" (Rev 3:20). Living in the presence of God, Who knocks on the door of your heart through daily events, is precisely what will allow you to be one of the blessed servants of whom Jesus says, "Blessed are those servants whom the master finds vigilant on his arrival. Amen, I say to you, he will gird himself, have them recline at table, and proceed to wait on them" (Lk 12:37).

Christ foretells what happens to the servant who is ready to meet Him: He will have him sit at His own place and so experience that which Christ Himself lives. Jesus promises man that He will allow him to live God's interior life to some degree. Even though the creature will never be like the Creator, the Lord wants to reveal to His faithful servant what is His deepest mystery: His interior life.

Christ promises to glorify your nature. This is what will happen in the life to come, in Heaven. But, if you want to live in the truth now, here on the earth, then you will be able to participate in the great mysteries of God's interior life through faith.

Slawomir Cezary Biela was born in Poland in 1956. He studied at the Warsaw University of Technology, where he earned his Doctorate in Physics. He also studied at the Papal Faculty of Theology in Warsaw, especially in the field of the Theology of Spirituality.

Since 1977, S. C. Biela has been cooperating very closely with Rev. Tadeusz Dajczer, Professor of Theology, who is also the founder of the Families of Nazareth Movement. Together, through countless and laborious efforts, they laid the foundation for the spirituality of this worldwide Movement.

Consequently, since 1986, Slawomir has been a member of the editorial team responsible for preparing various publications pertaining to the spiritual formation of the Movement's members. Because of their timely issues, these publications have been translated into fourteen languages.

The book *Behold, I Stand at the Door and Knock* is the fruit of the author's many years of deep reflections and insights regarding the Christian spiritual life. In it he expounds on and explains various stages of interior life. For this very reason his book can be beneficial for both the beginners in spiritual life, as well as those who are more advanced, leading them on their road to *transforming union with Christ*.

The book ***Behold, I Stand at the Door and Knock*** presents the same thrust or vein of spirituality as the author's other books, including his titles ***In the Arms of Mary*** (also known as ***Praying self-abandonment to Divine Love***) and ***God Alone Suffices***. It is worth noting that these particular books have been published in the following countries: USA, Canada, Great Britain, Ireland, the Philippines, South Korea, Spain, Mexico, Portugal, Brazil, Italy, Holland, Lithuania, Czech Republic, Bulgaria, Romania and Byelorussia. As of this printing, translations are being prepared in the following languages: German, French, Ukrainian, Latvian, Russian, Hungarian, Slovak, Albanian and Vietnamese.

Behold, I Stand at the Door and Knock presents the same spirituality as the worldwide best-seller ***Inquiring Faith*** (known in the USA as ***The Gift of Faith***), by Rev. Tadeusz Dajczer, who is mentioned above. ***The Gift of Faith*** is translated in over 40 languages.

BOOKS BY SLAWOMIR BIELA

IN THE ARMS OF MARY
ISBN 0-9721432-1-1
(a.k.a. PRAYING SELF-ABANDONMENT TO DIVINE LOVE)

This book is the fruit of S. C. Biela's many years of deep reflections and insights regarding the Christian spiritual life. In it he explains and refers to the various stages of one's interior life and offers a pathway to deepening one's prayer. For this very reason, *In the Arms of Mary* can serve as a resource for spiritual renewal both for beginners and those who are more advanced on the path toward a "transforming union with Christ."

GOD ALONE SUFFICES
ISBN 0-9721432-2-X

In this book S. C. Biela expounds on various ways that an individual can grow in his interior life by letting go of the illusions of this world, and replacing them with total reliance on God. The author guides his reader on a path toward complete surrender of self to the God of love.

BEHOLD, I STAND AT THE DOOR AND KNOCK
ISBN 0-9721432-3-8

"Behold, I stand at the door and knock. If anyone hears my voice and opens the door, [then] I will enter his house and dine with him, and he

with me" (Rev 3:20). This book leads the reader to discover the constant loving and merciful Presence of God. God never leaves His beloved children alone. He is always at the doors of our hearts knocking, awaiting our opening of ourselves to Him. Discover the different ways God knocks, why we hesitate to open the doors of our hearts, and what treasure lies ready for us when we do open the door to our Creator.

OPEN WIDE THE DOOR TO CHRIST
ISBN 0-9721432-7-0

Continuing the themes presented in *Behold, I Stand at the Door and Knock*, S. C. Biela helps to convince the reader of the treasure that awaits when, upon hearing Christ's knocking, we finally open wide the door to our Creator. He reminds us of the key: spiritual poverty. "Blessed are the poor in spirit, for theirs is the kingdom of heaven" (Mt 5:3). But how does one become poor in spirit? That is exactly what this book addresses. A must read for all who desire a "transforming union with Christ."

OTHER BOOKS IN THIS SPIRITUALITY

THE GIFT OF FAITH, by Father Tadeusz Dajczer
ISBN 0-9721432-0-3

An international bestseller in the field of Christian spirituality, this book about the interior life is a call to abandon oneself to God according to the Gospel edict: "unless you turn and become like children, you will not enter the kingdom of Heaven." With simplicity and clarity, the author manages to draw the reader's attention and awaken the yearning to experience God and to follow a specific path toward sanctity.

FOUNDATION

COMMUNION OF LIFE WITH CHRIST THROUGH MARY

IN THE ARMS OF MARY FOUNDATION
P.O. Box 271987
Fort Collins, CO 80527-1987

If *Behold, I Stand at the Door and Knock* has helped you to appreciate God's immense love and mercy, then consider donating to **In the Arms of Mary Foundation** to help in the spreading of this spirituality (Communion of life with Christ through Mary) throughout the U.S.A. and the world. Send checks or money orders payable to **In the Arms of Mary Foundation** to the above address.

For more information about the Foundation "In the Arms of Mary" or to obtain additional copies of this book, or other books on this spirituality, please visit our website at www.IntheArmsofMary.org.